Power to the Teacher

Published in Association with

PHI DELTA KAPPA

POWER

TO THE TEACHER

How America's Educators

Became Militant

Marshall O. Donley, Jr.

INDIANA UNIVERSITY PRESS

BLOOMINGTON / LONDON

Published in Canada by Fitzhenry & Whiteside Limited, Don Mills, Ontario

Manufactured in the United States of America

Library of Congress Cataloging in Publication Data

Donley, Marshall O 1932–
    Power to the teacher.

    Bibliography
    Includes index.
    1. Educational associations—United States—History.
2. Teachers' unions—United States—History.
I. Title.
L13.A2D66   1976   331.88′11′371100973   75-31421
ISBN 0-253-34562-6
ISBN 0-253-20194-2 pbk.   1 2 3 4 5 80 79 78 77 76

To MILDRED SANDISON FENNER REID,
whose sense of history helped to develop mine.

CONTENTS

PREFACE

PARTS AND PIECES have been told of the story of America's teachers and how they organized during the two hundred years of the Republic. Henry Barnard's *American Journals of Education* tell much about schools and schoolmen in the 1800s. Histories of education in the United States have been written, as well as histories of the National Education Association, the American Federation of Teachers, state and local teachers unions and associations. No one, however, had brought this story together or analyzed its meaning.

In the mid-1960s, as part of a doctoral program at the American University in Washington, D.C., I began to take a broad historical look at the nation's teachers and at how they organized to improve their lot and to better public education. Readers interested in a detailed study of the teacher movement between 1850 and 1968 can find it in my dissertation, *A Study of the Roots, Causes, and Directions of Teacher Militancy in the United States.*

This present volume abridges the historical material in the dissertation, extends the history of teacher activism into the 1970s, and offers insights into reasons teachers organized, how their unions and associations evolved, and where teachers and their groups are headed.

As an editor and writer in the field of teacher organizing

during the past years, I have seen teacher activism gain momentum and power. As a result of this experience, much of the material in this book is based on direct knowledge of the events and the people who shaped them. My journalistic training has enabled me, I hope, to maintain an independent, interpretive view of these events, though I accept the blame for any prejudices that appear, as I do for the validity of my projections.

In writing this book, I have felt the debt I owe to those professors at American University who guided my doctoral work (especially Paul D. Leedy) and to my wife, Margaret Reagan Donley, whose editorial guidance and technical assistance have been invaluable. My final debt, of course, is to the teachers in America's public schools. Their struggle to serve both the pupils of the nation and their own needs for dignity and security has taught me many lessons in perseverance, humility, and faith.

INTRODUCTION

ONE OF THE UNIQUE contributions of American democracy to world history is its system of public education. Throughout much of its two hundred years, the United States has developed and its people have supported schools for the masses. Other nations have educated their elite; America has attempted to school all its children. Some nations have schooled solely for the goals of the state; America has schooled mainly for the development of the self. Often forgotten in this record of achievement are the artisans who fashioned it—the teachers. In the cold, one-room schools of colonial New England, on shady porches in the antebellum South, in Spanish mission schools, teachers molded minds and hearts. In Lancastrian schools of the mid-nineteenth century, in academies of the early twentieth century, and in comprehensive high schools of the present, they have offered literacy and learning to the young.

These teachers—their struggles and their idealism—are the focus of this book. Theirs is a story of growth from individual poverty and helplessness to group activism for decent pay and status. Between 1841 and the Civil War, the wages of men teachers ranged from $4.15 to $6.30 weekly in rural areas, from $11.93 to $18.07 in the cities. Women got less. Teachers were not thought deserving of more remuneration; some did not even hope for more. In the words of a normal school teacher in

1839, "It is not to be expected that teaching will ever become a *lucrative* position." The behavior of these poorly paid servants, in school and out, was both prescribed and proscribed by the community. Special rules regarding smoking, drinking, courting, and church-going were strictly enforced, even to the point of limiting the right of teachers to leave town without permission. In the South, teachers sometimes actually were slaves—literate blacks assigned the task of imparting the ABCs to the white children on the plantation. Some teachers rankled under the limits of their status, but most did not. Those unable to endure the restraints moved on, if they could, to other jobs; for many, teaching was a starting point for other professions, a way to earn a few dollars until better prospects turned up.

This servant status began to change when teachers sought to organize, when they found the strength that lies in unity. An 1850s Illinois teachers' society noted, "Group petitions got a readier response from school boards than did the individual requests from the teacher." A union of educators could act where a lone schoolmaster could not. As more and more joined together to focus on mutual problems, their power grew; their salaries increased; and they won new rights and responsibilities in American society.

Power to the Teacher

1 / The Teacher Alone

D URING THE SPRING OF 1974, in the town of Hortonville, Wisconsin, schoolteachers were marching with picket signs. They chanted their demands and, when restrained by specially named deputy sheriffs, they swung their signs as weapons. Representatives of other public employees joined their picket lines and went to jail along with dozens of teachers when the deputies arrested demonstrators. Hortonville's teachers were struggling to force a recalcitrant school board to bargain collectively; they were putting their jobs on the line for the values of collective action. And they were not alone. Colleagues in other towns, other states joined their fight, sent them money for subsistence and legal fees, mailed them letters of support.

The Hortonville strike, not unusual for the 1970s, would have horrified American teachers of earlier eras. Militant actions by teachers were exceedingly rare during the colonial years and the first 150 years of the Republic. The few instances on record show individual teachers acting within the context of untenable situations. For example, in 1666 Ezekiel Cheever, who had established a "Town Free School" in Charlestown,

Massachusetts, found himself in unusually tight financial straits. His pittance of a salary had not been paid on schedule, schools in nearby towns had lured away some of his pupils, and his schoolhouse was falling apart. Cheever spoke up at a town council meeting and by his audacity persuaded the selectmen to promise that they would "take care the schoolhouse be speedily amended because it is much out of repair" and see to it that his yearly salary was paid (the constables, he told them, being "much behind him"). Cheever also won their promise that no other schoolmaster would "be suffered or set up in the town."

Another instance of "militancy" took place during the 1790s elsewhere in Massachusetts. Schoolmaster Caleb Bingham was a modest and, usually, a timid man. But the town fathers had not paid him or the other teachers for months. Instead, they were handed a paper certifying that the town owed them a certain sum. These certificates or "town orders" could then be sold at the bank for a considerable discount. Bingham decided he had had enough. When he received his next certificate, he advertised it for sale in the town newspaper, in effect publicizing the fiscal state of the community. This public insult led to a town meeting, to which Bingham was summoned by a constable. Called on for his apology, Bingham gave a brief account of his frustrations. "I have a family and need the money," he explained. "I have done my part of the engagement faithfully, and have no apology to make to those who have failed to do theirs. All I can do is to promise that if the town will punctually pay my salary in the future, I will never advertise their orders for sale again." Reportedly the town treasurer slapped him on the shoulder and said, "Bingham, you are a good fellow; call at my office after the meeting and I will give you the cash." Presumably, Bingham had no further trouble collecting what was due him.

In 1802 Thomas Peugh, a teacher in a settlement north of Cincinnati, "refused to unlock the school and hold class until such time as the school committee formally committed to paper a stipulation giving him at least one afternoon per month

4

off so that he might move to his new lodging." And in 1823 Connecticut teacher William A. Alcott wrote a long and stormy series for the New Haven *Columbia Register*, telling of the failures of common school education in his town of Wolcott. He evidently hoped the publicity of the newspaper items would stimulate his employers to improve the condition of his schoolroom, but the townsmen held stubbornly to their pocketbooks and no improvements were made. When Alcott asked for schoolroom seats with backs on them, the town leaders just stared at him.

How many other teachers demanded improved schools or due salaries is unknown, but the number was probably small. Until at least the early 1900s the typical teacher was humble and uncomplaining. He was expected to be religiously ortho-dox, loyal to the government, and morally acceptable. A Massachusetts law of 1654, for example, required that the overseers of Harvard and the selectmen of the towns discourage the employment of teachers "unsound in the faith or scandal-ous in their lives." Like the minister, the teacher was expected to provide a moral example for the children in his care. Each community maintained a continuous interest in the behavior of its teachers both in and out of school. And the teachers themselves, nearly all of them, accepted their state. When in 1863 California's teachers created a publication to speak for them, it was from a desire "to make known the spirit and the purpose which characterize their teaching. Humble in its position and appearance, like the profession of which it is to be the organ, this journal aims . . . to aid the future by making the school better, the teachers more genial, contented, and wise. . . ."

THE QUIESCENT TEACHER

So the acts of Ezekiel Cheever, Caleb Bingham, Thomas Peugh, and William A. Alcott were not typical. More common was the quiescence of the teachers at Lane Theological Seminary in Cincinnati. These teachers, when the 1837 depression crippled the schools' resources, "clung to their posts, although without private resources, and, by resolute though distressing self-sacrifice, maintained the operations of the institution until better times returned, and their scanty incomes were partially restored."

The rural teacher faced an even worse fate, dependent as he was on the vagaries of a farming economy. "In consequence of the scanty harvest of 1848," a Utah historian reported, "breadstuffs and other provisions became very scarce in the valley in the summer of 1849, and many of the people were necessitated to eat raw hides and to dig sego and thistle roots for months. Under such circumstance, one can understand why foods would be more important . . . than money. During the first years, it was common for teachers to accept 'valley produce' for their teaching in lieu of money." Some teachers preferred their pay in cash, but arrangements could be made to pay in produce. Advertisements like the one by Elib Kelsey in 1852 were common. He asserted that he proposed to open a day school and would accept pupils on the following terms: "For spelling, reading, writing, and arithmetic, $5. . . . The produce of the Valley will be taken in payment for tuition in all cases; when the terms of payment are not agreed upon, cash will be expected."

Rural or urban, the schoolmaster of the 1800s found working conditions rugged and salaries meager. He was caught in a vicious circle: his low pay branded him a second-class citizen, while low esteem hindered his efforts to obtain greater compensation. His situation especially rankled in a society that placed strong emphasis on individual economic success. Gradually, however, as public schools grew in number and attendance, educators began to form groups. The value of organizing rarely has been so lauded as by J. W. Bulkley, Brooklyn superintendent of schools. Speaking in 1864 before the nascent National Teachers Association, he declared:

The great principle of association was first enunciated by the Creator in Eden, when the Lord God said, "It is *not* good that man

6

shall be alone." In the family, the tribe, the state, the nation; we find this great truth exemplified. All history, sacred and profane, develop [sic] this idea clearly. In the history and progress of civilization, we find that just in proportion to the perfection of this bond that binds man to his fellow, in the community; also in united effort for the development of a given theory, whether in government, science, art, or literature, strength is found for the accomplishment of anything within the range of human possibility. In educational reform, this principle is indispensable to success. Isolated effort has accomplished much in every department of life. But what is individual compared with associated effort?

2 / Teachers Organize

THE NATION'S FIRST TEACHERS ASSOCIATION, the Society of Associated Teachers of New York City, was established in 1794. Five years later the School Association of the County of Middlesex, Connecticut, was founded. The Associated Instructors of Youth in the Town of Boston and Its Vicinity survived for a few years following 1812. County-wide and city-wide groups were set up in many states, and between 1840 and 1861, thirty state teachers associations were formed. The birth of these groups was attended by a kind of schizophrenia that has continued into the present. From the first, educators were torn between their desire to promote and improve public education and their determination to better their own conditions. In view of their genteel respectability, they could not very well strive only for the latter. Thus, teachers groups have been strained and occasionally torn apart by conflicting needs to serve society and to serve self.

This dichotomy of purpose is evident in early records of teacher groups. During the 1860s, for example, State Superintendent William R. White told West Virginia Education

Association members that they should make teaching the business of their lives, nurture the missionary spirit, and follow their vocation whether or not they were adequately rewarded financially. Many spoke up to oppose this view, and one member asked if any person present would not give up teaching if he could make more money doing something else. When another member said he knew a young man who had refused to give up teaching for a more lucrative position, a voice from the back called out, "Barnum ought to have that man." After much debate, the consensus was that teachers were afflicted as much with a hankering after the "mammon of unrighteousness" as other people. At the first meeting of the New York State Teachers Association, the group's secretary urged educators to join for "the welfare of our schools, the defense of the individual and the professional character, as well as obligations to our country." The letters of invitation to the meeting showed the other side of the coin, however, calling for an increase in "the pay and influence of those engaged in this arduous and honorable profession."

Altruism accounted for much of the fluctuation of teacher groups between welfare concerns and the drive for better public education. Some members sincerely believed that advances for teachers would follow automatically when the public realized that it should support the schools more adequately. Only a few believed that higher pay for teachers could precede a great improvement in the quality of teachers themselves. Did the appearance of the normal school with its better-trained product come first and persuade communities to pay higher and more equitable salaries? Or did the public first commence to pay salaries that justified the investment by young men and women in the longer normal school training? David Perkins Page, principal of New York's first normal school at Albany, who discussed this problem in 1847 in his *Theory and Practice of Teaching*, concluded that the two factors must go hand in hand. If a priority had to be assigned, however, Perkins thought improvement in teaching should come first.

9

Another reason for the dichotomy was one that would remain a source of conflict in teacher groups for a century: the dominance of these groups by superintendents and college administrators. The practical teacher himself rarely was a leader in "his" association. Women—soon to be a majority in the profession—were even unable to become full members of most educators groups. A South Dakota historian, telling of the problems of low teacher pay in the nineteenth century, commented, "Maybe if there had been more classroom teachers participating in early deliberations, they would have created a different attitude from that manifested by an [association] dominated by school administrators, who were probably faring relatively well themselves in the way of salaries." In Tennessee, as elsewhere, classroom teachers were conspicuously absent as association members. In 1865 teachers were an almost negligible minority of the state group; most members were legislators, college presidents, and other prominent persons.

A NATIONAL ASSOCIATION

When a national teachers group was formed in 1857, the invitation called on all "practical teachers" to assemble in Philadelphia "for the purpose of organizing a National Teachers Association." The invitations were mailed not to teachers, however, but to the presidents of the state education associations, ten of whom accepted. Forty-three educators attended the organizing meeting, but few of them were classroom practitioners. Total membership in the national group never topped three hundred until the 1870s, when the organization merged with the National Association of School Superintendents and the American Normal School Association, both of which became departments of what was then called the National Educational Association.

These limited numbers and the disproportionate supervisory and college membership hampered the new association, as did the members' tendency to talk a lot and do little. As one sociologist said, "Professors are the greatest talkers in the world, but they are no kind of doers at all. . . . Talkers are notoriously slow and ill-organized doers." Another observer, James Cruickshank, reported this conversation with William McAndrew:

"And how long before you advanced from high-hat meetings to the practical improvement of teachers?" asked McAndrew.

"Gradually. There was, at the start, too much *why*, not enough *what*, and hardly any *how* at all. Even the most practical schoolmen, when asked to prepare addresses, suffered an attack of pedantry and soared to cloudland."

This propensity to talk, mainly about important-sounding matters, dominated the first decades of the national association. William T. Harris, who personally gave 145 speeches before the group, in 1891 classified the speeches delivered from 1858 through 1890. His effort revealed that the major topics had little to do with practical improvement in the teachers' lot. The favorite topic in those years was theory and psychology, followed closely by high schools and colleges, normal schools, manual training and technical schools, courses of study, kindergartens, primary grades, music education, moral and religious instruction, and philosophy of methods. The certification, preparation, and requirements of teachers received frequent and constant attention; but specifics, like tenure, salary, status, and conditions, did not come to the fore until the 1920s.

The purposes of the national association, like those of state groups, were dual: to upgrade both public education and teaching conditions—in the words of its charter, "To elevate the character and advance the interests of the profession of teaching, and to promote the cause of popular education in the United States." So the national association found itself, from the first, facing the same dichotomy as did the state groups: a concern for improving conditions for teachers, but either unwilling or unable to press for them until the more general goal of better schooling had been met. NTA President John D. Philbrick reinforced this view at the 1863 annual meeting:

11

One of the principal means of elevating the character of teachers is to increase the demand for accomplished teachers. And this demand will be increased as the progress of education is advanced and its value is appreciated. After all that can be done for the improvement of education, it is substantially what the teachers make it. The stream cannot rise higher than its foundation. . . . The proper means should be employed to secure continued self-improvement of teachers; and with this view they should, as far as practicable, be commended, promoted, and rewarded in proportion to their advancement, and degraded or removed for delinquency and neglect of duty.

Thirty-one years later, a woman principal challenged Philbrick's ideas in an address at the 1894 annual meeting of the national association. She said, "If I were to ask what you consider the noblest work in which a man can engage, you would probably reply, that in which he can do the most good for mankind. On vote, I believe the work of the teacher would stand first, and yet, is this a profession which you desire your son to follow? I think not. Why is this? What is lacking? Largely, to my mind, it is a matter of dollars and cents. When the profession of teaching pays as well as do the other professions, there will be more strong young men attracted to it—when special proficiency receives special pecuniary compensation."

SOME GAINS

Teacher groups did make gains before 1900. Despite the heavy obstacles—limited membership, nebulous discussions, commitment to overall improvement in the schools before teachers' benefits, and dominance by nonteachers—the national association could point to one major success: the formation of a federal Department of Education. State associations, meanwhile, were becoming involved in some practical changes. The Illinois Education Association helped to establish the common school fund supported by a two-mill property tax

(1853–55). It promoted the establishment of kindergartens and secured an enabling act for this purpose (1895). The association also helped to secure constitutional mandate for free schools for all children (1870) and to establish the state's first normal schools (1853–57). The New Hampshire Education Association recommended a free textbook bill to the legislature (1887), backed the first compulsory school attendance law (1872), and worked to establish the first normal school in its state (1870). The New Mexico Education Association secured taxation of district property for support of schools (1891). The New York State Teachers Association proposed a uniform system of licensing for teachers in 1887; a written licensing examination was instituted the next year. The New Jersey Association, before 1900, had begun, in its words, "activities in the major fields that were to occupy it for the next quarter-century—retirement, tenure, and minimum salary—and growing out of them a vigorous program of legal defense of teachers whose rights as teachers were threatened." The West Virginia Education Association inaugurated a campaign in 1891 for higher salaries: "Teachers throughout the state should labor to increase their salaries. Justice in this respect cannot be secured by mere complaint; no reform was ever achieved in this way. The thing to do is to organize and take steps to present the question to the people."

Although other examples could be added, more important than these immediate efforts of the associations was the fact that they had been formed. That they were organized was their first and most basic contribution to the militancy of teachers. Here was a potential forum. Association offices held by superintendents could and would be held later by teachers. Convention topics could and would be changed from discussing theories to planning actions. The founding of teacher groups had made available a mechanism; it needed only to be put to work.

Also contributing to teacher militancy before the turn of the century were two bellwether events. During 1880 in

Pennsylvania, eight schoolteachers went on strike for an advance in wages. And in 1897 the Chicago Teachers Federation was formed. Although not yet affiliated with organized labor, the federation pointed to another route for teacher militancy.

3 / Hints of Things
to Come

THE FIRST 20 YEARS of the twentieth century brought no sudden increase in teacher militancy. Although the period was one of industrial and civil strife, for teachers it was generally just more of the same—low pay, low status, and little opportunity to make changes. A few teacher actions, however, hinted of things to come.

In 1904 a group of Illinois teachers won a salary victory. In February that year, the Saline County Teachers Association appointed a committee to study salaries. The committee examined the assessment records in the office of the county clerk, considered the number of pupils enrolled in the various schools, and prepared a schedule calling for minimum salaries from $25 to $100 a month. When this schedule was mailed to every teacher in the county, with a request that he stand by the committee's demands, the school directors complained bitterly, but the sentiment of the county supported the teachers. Only fifteen of 125 teachers accepted positions at less than the scheduled rate, and some boards paid $10 or $15 above the scheduled minimum. After the increase, the average monthly salary of men in Saline County was $45 and of women $40.

School administrators and college people immediately reacted against the idea of teachers organizing to enforce demands. Illinois State Normal University's president commented on the teachers' victory: "Under modern industrial conditions has almost entirely disappeared the human sympathy that under an earlier system bound together master and man in a common interest. Who would teach if the same spirit of antagonism is to reign in the relations of teacher and the community which they serve? So, I take it, we shall resort to no trades-union methods. We shall continue to present our claims with dignity and moderation, confident that the sense of justice and the generous disposition of the American people will give them due recognition." Judging by the few instances of teacher activism at that time, his attitude was far more typical than that of the 125 Saline County teachers.

In 1908 some Virginia teachers pioneered a route teachers would take increasingly: They held a mass rally in public to emphasize a cause. In a Virginia county supervision campaign that year, the state teachers group, through its local affiliates, sponsored rallies of teachers, school officials, and citizens in every county. In 1916, teachers in Scranton, Pennsylvania, carried out what was probably the first successful teachers' political campaign in the nation's history. The Scranton Teachers Association was formed as a result of a mass meeting of grade teachers to protest having to take a written examination on McMurray's *How to Study*. Apparently the next year's contracts were to include salaries based on scores on this test. The Scranton union, affiliated with the American Federation of Labor, sought an injunction to prevent the superintendent from conducting the examination. Further, the teachers decided to take an active part in the fall school board elections. They campaigned for candidates they favored and succeeded in electing one member to the school board.

In New York City, a teachers union organized in 1916

16

made its first order of business an attempt to raise salaries. The union held a mass rally, at which the secretary-treasurer said that a 47.8 percent average increase in salaries would be needed to restore teachers' purchasing power to the 1912 level. The rally and subsequent attempts failed, though, and New York school conditions changed little until after World War I. Further, the union was constantly under attack, new burdens were imposed on teachers, and an attempt was made to lengthen the school day.

One teacher strike took place between 1900 and World War I. In 1918, teachers of Memphis, Tennessee, walked out, demanding a 33⅓ percent salary increase. The Memphis school board countered with an offer of $10 more a month and the strike was settled.

Low Pay and Status

These actions were few and far between. As a rule, during the first 20 years of this century, poorly paid and ill-prepared, the American teacher gained little money and less respect from society. He was still expected to be cheerful, meek, loyal, and most of all, quiet. Indicative was the reaction of the New York superintendent of schools when, in 1905, he was asked if there were no conditions which might justify a teacher in complaining of his superior. The superintendent's answer: "Absolutely none." Nor was teaching thought by many to be a profession. Fassett A. Cotton, Indiana state superintendent of public instruction, expressed such doubts in 1906 in the fiftieth anniversary volume of the National Educational Association. He said:

After all, one of the greatest causes of poor pay to teachers is the fact that the vast majority of teachers are not professional educators. The calling is still a stepping-stone to other professions and will continue to be so as long as present conditions exist. The prospective lawyer, doctor, or minister are willing to take temporary employment as a teacher at a lower salary than a professional

17

educator can afford to take it. There is a great deal in the attitude of consciousness with which one comes to a calling. Men enter law and medicine for life. The average life of the teacher is four years. It is safe to say that a large percentage of those who teach on and on do so in yearly anticipation of some change for the better that may come to their relief. Many are teaching because they had not the profession of their choice. Many others are teaching because they had not the means to go into business. Poverty makes teachers subservient to society. They get used to small means and small ways, and for this reason are incapacitated for the big things in life.

Others warned teachers that they should not pursue self-interest in any case. An editorial in the *Western Journal of Education* told them in 1907: "The increase of salaries, the tenure of positions, the pension of teachers, the standard of certification should come from the intelligent citizens of the commonwealth, not from the schoolmasters. But the schoolmaster in his association and his organization for power, should stand for the highest ideals of professional ethics, for standards in mental processes, for standards of teaching, for the development of the child, for expert educational work. The schoolmaster should lead in educational ideals, but the parents must lead in the material welfare of the teacher." For gains in benefits, the editorial went on, teachers still had to rely on "a very clear demonstration to the public that such action is absolutely necessary for the good of the children and consequently for society; the material comfort of the teachers, apart from their efficiency for educational work, must always be a minor factor in the eyes of the public."

Although teachers' salaries were pitifully low throughout the nation, educational leaders reassured teachers that prospects were good. William T. Harris, U.S. Commissioner of Education, told teachers in 1905: "The teacher whose salary is low . . . will try to improve his skill in teaching. . . . He will study to perfect himself in fine manners. He will pass under review his moral judgments. . . . What teacher could not improve his position and find a more adequate salary for

18

himself? . . . There is, in fact, a great lack in number and quality for the highest positions and best salaries that are offered in the United States. . . . The future of teachers' salaries is, therefore, a bright and promising one."

NEA Debates

From 1900 through 1919, the National Education Association (the *al* was dropped from *Education* in 1906 when the association received a charter from Congress) basically continued its role as in the preceding century. It was primarily a debating society—a place where educational ideas could be aired. The NEA secretary in 1905, for example, made no efforts to advance the benefits of teachers. He spent most of his time keeping all records of the association, editing, proofreading, and distributing *Proceedings*, collecting dues, keeping a complete system of books, and negotiating arrangements with railway associations for rates and ticket conditions to the convention. The NEA continued to hold its annual conventions and to discuss the traditional topics, apparently thinking it beneath the dignity of the association to talk about the money basis of education. Membership in the group remained very low during this period, both in absolute numbers and in percentage of the teaching force. The 2,332 members in 1900 represented 0.6 percent of the classroom teachers in public schools. By 1910 this number had grown to 6,909, representing 1.3 percent of the teaching force.

Although few direct actions were taken by NEA, some dramatic and interesting ideas were expressed before this national forum. Margaret A. Haley, president of the National Federation of Teachers, probed some of the myths about the profession at the 1904 annual meeting. First she examined the idea that teachers should depend on an educated public to generously give up largess for the schools and schoolteachers:

If the American people cannot be made to realize and meet their responsibilities to the public school, no self-appointed custodians of the public intelligence and conscience can do it for them. Horace Mann, speaking of the dependence of the prosperity of the schools on the public intelligence, said, "The people will sustain no better schools and have no better education than they personally see the need of; and, therefore, the people are to be informed and elevated as a preliminary step toward elevating the schools." Sometimes, in our impatience at the slowness with which the public moves in these matters, we are tempted to disregard this wise counsel.

Then she challenged the idea that the teacher should limit efforts for self-improvement until the school and the child are bettered: "There is no possible conflict between the interest of the child and the interest of the teacher. . . . For both the child and the teacher, freedom is the condition of development. The atmosphere in which it is easiest to teach is the atmosphere in which it is easiest to learn. The same things that are a burden to the teacher are a burden also to the child. The same things which restrict her powers restrict his powers also."

President Haley also spoke out against the railroad and corporation lobbies that reach "to the legislatures and to the taxing bodies—yes, even to the bench—and in whose hands these servants of the people are as wax and obey the command of the lobby, and defy the law they were elected and sworn to uphold." Organized efforts of teachers could challenge this type of anarchy, she said. Finally, she challenged the idea that labor and education must remain separate. Not at all, she said, for

there is no possible conflict between the good of society and the good of its members, of which the industrial workers are the vast majority. . . . If there is one body of public servants of whom the public has the right to expect the mental and moral equipment to face the labor question . . . it is the public school teachers. . . . The essential thing is that the public school teachers recognize the fact that their struggles to maintain the efficiency of the schools through better conditions for themselves is part of the same great struggle which the manual workers . . . have been making for humanity . . . and that lack of the unfavorable conditions of both is a common cause.

Other hints of teacher militancy appeared in speeches at NEA meetings during this prewar period. Speakers began to suggest that teachers, in contrast to superintendents and school board members, should have some role in guiding the policies of the schools. Miss Haley alluded to this idea by quoting John Dewey, who in 1903 urged that "the public school system [be] organized in such a way that every teacher has some regular and representative way in which he or she can register judgment upon matters of educational importance with the assurance that this judgment will somehow affect the school system." Ella Flagg Young, principal of the Chicago Normal School, and destined to be NEA's first woman president, made a similar point in 1907. Speaking before the National Council of Education (an NEA subgroup), she said: "If the public school system is to meet the demands which twentieth century civilization would lay upon it, the isolation of the great body of teachers from the administration of the school must be overcome. Can it be possible that the teachers in the great public school system have not that poise of mind and interest in education which would make them valuable counselors? Or, on the other hand, can it be true that teachers are stronger in their work when they have no voice in the planning of the great issues committed to their hands?" At the association's 1919 annual meeting, Mary C. Harris of Minneapolis reported the forming of a Teachers Educational Council in that city to bridge the gap between teachers and administrators. Although the council was advisory, she said, it "has dealt with such vital problems as courses of study, textbooks, the merit system, length of day, typical school building, and salary increases."

Throughout this period, the National Education Association's concern for improved salaries and other benefits for teachers was expressed in two ways. First, nearly every year the members would pass a resolution calling for higher salaries. Typical of these resolutions is the one approved in 1915:

Recognizing that in the last analysis the excellence of our public schools depends upon the teachers who do the actual work of instruction, this Association believes it is of the highest importance that this work be done under the best possible conditions as to the promotion of good health, comfort, and peace of mind. To this end the Association expresses itself unequivocally in favor of adequate salaries, security of tenure, a suitable retirement annuity, and working conditions in which there shall be sufficient and helpful supervision; and at the same time freedom from arbitrary or needless restrictions or requirements, and from those "ratings" and records which unnecessarily disturb the teacher's peace and make the rendering of the best service impossible.

Second, the association inaugurated a series of salary studies. In 1905 the first, a 466-page document, recorded the pay of teachers in nearly all cities with a population greater than 8,000 and included the salaries of teachers in selected smaller towns and rural areas. Further, the study suggested ways funds could be raised to pay higher salaries; it proposed minimum salary laws, compared costs of living around the nation, and compared earnings of teachers and other workers. Association committees prepared additional salary reports in 1913, 1914, 1918, and 1919.

Some NEA members were beginning to ask themselves if the group should start to work publicly and actively for higher salaries and other benefits. A blueprint for such action was offered in 1913 by Harry Suzzallo, professor of the philosophy of education at Teachers College, Columbia University. Suzzallo suggested, "The need is for a more adequate national organization of all American public school teachers upon a permanent basis which will insure a day-to-day influence upon school affairs." Making it clear that he was not proposing a national teachers union, he called for the "ethical cooperation" of the 500,000 Americans who were then in the teaching profession. Suzzallo laid out detailed plans for local teachers associations (with active and associate members), state education associations, and a national council of state education associations, with unified dues paid from the local and each level affiliated with the others. "The primary purpose of such

22

organization," Suzzallo said, "is to increase the efficiency of education as a public service" and "as a mode of attaining this chief end, its secondary purpose is to improve the status of teachers." Suzzallo further suggested some goals for this unified organization: improving the economic status of teachers through a minimum salary system, 12-month payment for teachers, increases in salaries above the increased cost of living, and a statewide pension system.

Suzzallo's ideas lay fallow for four years while World War I captured the attention of teachers and other citizens. As the war continued, and as America's industries and large numbers of persons became involved in it, a rapid inflation rocked the nation. It hit teachers especially hard and brewed among them a deeply rooted unrest because their salaries had not been adjusted to keep pace with wartime living costs. This unrest became one of two forces that led to a massive growth in the National Education Association. The second force was J. W. Crabtree, a Nebraska educator who was hired as NEA's secretary in September, 1917. Crabtree fully accepted Suzzallo's ideas and set as his first task a membership campaign to make NEA representative of classroom teachers. Thus the "political teacher" at last started hearing the voice of the National Education Association; it was speaking now about a topic of vital interest to him: his pocketbook.

State Associations

NEA membership in the first 20 years of the twentieth century was tiny, with fewer than 7 percent of all educators enrolled by 1919. State education associations, though, did better. By 1907 they had enrolled 14 percent of employed teachers in their states; by 1916 they had enrolled 34 percent, which amounted to 188,730 educators, a much greater number than joined the national association. It is not surprising, then, that much of the work on behalf of teachers during this period continued to be carried on by state groups. They encouraged legislatures to provide tenure and job security for teachers; they pressed for better teachers' salaries, usually by urging passage of minimum wage laws; they backed legislation to establish teachers' retirement systems; they set up codes of ethics for teachers; and at least one association provided legal defense for a teacher during this period.

The first tenure act for educators in the nation became law in New Jersey in 1908. The New Jersey Education Association claims credit for passage of the law, and describes it as the "nation's first and strongest teacher tenure law, protecting teachers and principals after three years against dismissal or reduction of salary except for proof of inefficiency, incapacity, or conduct unbecoming a teacher." In 1913, Montana's education association initiated and supported a "continuous contract" law for teachers. Massachusetts teachers worked for a statewide tenure law, and one was passed in 1914. The New York State Teachers Association worked for passage of such a law in 1917.

To establish minimum salaries for teachers was the goal of several state teacher groups in the first 20 years of the century, though few achieved this goal. In 1902 New Jersey members passed a resolution calling for a minimum salary law and establishing a committee to pursue it. A $450 annual minimum was suggested, but the state legislature failed to act on the proposal. Utah teachers worked for such a law, but again without success. A bit later, though, three state groups won passage of minimum salary laws. The Iowa State Education Association reported that the Iowa legislature passed a bill in 1913 "establishing minimum wages for teachers based upon the average grades on their certificates." The same year, West Virginia teachers' efforts were rewarded by legislation increasing minimum salaries to $75, $60, and $45 monthly. The minimums were so low, however, that when the state group met the following year its members urged higher ones. In 1918 the Massachusetts Teachers Association secured the state's first minimum salary law.

Teacher groups were more successful in promoting the establishment of retirement funds to pay their pensions. A New Jersey law, passed in 1910, was upheld by the state supreme court in 1911; a test case had appealed the failure of the Passaic school board to deduct retirement money from teachers' salaries. Illinois, Minnesota, and New Hampshire reported passage of retirement acts in 1915. And in 1917 the Pennsylvania State Education Association successfully lobbied its legislature to approve a retirement act. The West Virginia association worked for a pension law in 1912 and 1917, but the bill failed both times, though in 1917 one of the houses of the legislature passed it. In 1919 a law was passed permitting boards of education to set up pension plans.

Codes of ethics for teachers were adopted by eight state associations by 1920: Georgia was the first (1896), California second (1902), and Alabama third (1908). The codes urged the teacher to live by high standards of conduct, to recognize that the child's welfare was his major obligation, and to cooperate with his associates. Some of the codes suggested, furthermore, that teachers as well as administrators should have a role in developing and carrying out school policies. This early idea of teacher involvement in policy making foreshadowed a more meaningful role for teachers when negotiation agreements between school boards and teacher groups began to be written.

An early instance of another teacher role that was destined to expand occurred in 1911 in New Jersey. The state group financed legal aid for a member, a school principal who lost his position when the borough in which his school was located separated from the township that had hired him. The new political unit refused to uphold his contract, and a court case ensued. In discussing the case, one New Jersey leader pointed out, "The average teacher is utterly unable financially to prosecute or defend a suit. This Association is powerful financially and morally. It is its *duty*, it ought to be its *joy*, to fight the just battles of its members."

So state teacher groups pointed to a number of concrete

efforts on behalf of their members between 1900 and 1920. Some claims were exaggerated, however. For example, the legislation that teacher groups claimed to influence did not always owe its passage to their action. In many cases, legislation of interest to teachers was also vigorously pursued by the state department of education, which had more influence. In the opinion of many, including some prominent in state teacher groups, associations exerted little influence in legislative matters. One reason for this relative ineffectiveness in influencing laws was the inexperience and disinterest of teachers themselves in such efforts. Typical was an Iowa teachers legislative committee whose members saw as their greatest difficulty the arousal of the interest and cooperation of their fellows. "It is not the province of this committee to advocate the formation of teachers' unions," they said, "but there is no doubt that we ought to organize in some manner and make our organization felt as a power for good."

Unionism did have appeal for teachers in the big cities, however. It is in Chicago that the history of American teachers unions traditionally begins. The Chicago Teachers Federation was formed in 1897 and affiliated with the Chicago labor council in 1902. At that time, Chicago teachers faced the combined opposition of business, industry, a corrupt school board, and subservient newspapers. Margaret Haley, the Chicago teachers' leader, had found out earlier that the Chicago union labor council would stand with her in exposing corruption. She carried this point of view to the teachers, who accepted the labor support and went on to expose the corrupt school system and to make significant gains.

TEACHER UNIONS

The first group of teachers to affiliate with labor, however, was not in Chicago, but in San Antonio, Texas. The Texas teachers affiliated directly with the American Federation of Labor on September 29, 1902. Chicago teachers "went

26

labor" later the same year, but they affiliated with the city labor council, not directly with the national labor group.

The first call to organize a national teachers union went from *The American Teacher*, a publication which later became the official journal of the American Federation of Teachers. In January, 1913, the journal lamented, "Twice within a month recently it was the special humiliation of a member of the staff of this paper to have to listen to public speakers who remarked that they were speaking for the teachers, who hadn't the courage to speak for themselves." In its next issue (February, 1913) the journal included "A Call To Organize":

On the ground that teachers do the everyday work of teaching, and understand the conditions necessary for better teaching, we propose the following principles for new organization: Teachers should have a voice and a vote in the determination of educational policies. Teachers may justly claim the right to seats in the Board of Education, for the reason that they only can bring first-hand information to the representatives of the people concerning the actual working of the education system. . . . We advocate the adoption of a plan that will permit all the teachers to have a share in the administration of the affairs of their own schools.

This call for an organizational meeting was abortive, however. It was not until three years later that AFT was organized. This time the call was made by the Chicago Federation of Men Teachers, one of three Chicago teachers unions. On June 1, 1915, this group urged a meeting in the summer to plan a national union of teachers. After several delays, one union of teachers in nearby Gary, Indiana, responded. The three Chicago unions and the Gary teachers met April 15, 1916. When the numbers increased to eight unions by May 9, the American Federation of Teachers was formed. It would survive a rocky road in the coming years to take on what it called "the vital task of actually winning concrete advances for the welfare of classroom teachers."

4 / Classroom Teachers

to the Fore

IN THE ERA between the World Wars, despite a rash of teacher strikes in at least six states, most teachers not in the large cities or the coal-mining towns of Pennsylvania could be described only as broke, feminine, and inconspicuous. The classic sociological study of the period, the Lynds' *Middletown*, describes the status of Muncie, Indiana, teachers:

In the school as in the home, child-training is largely left to the womenfolk. Four-fifths of Middletown's teachers are women, the majority of them unmarried women under 40. . . . Middletown pays its teachers more than it did 35 years ago, but even the $2,100 maximum paid to the grade school principals and high school teachers, the $3,200 paid to the high school principal, and the $4,900 to the superintendent of schools are hardly enough to tempt many of the abler men away from business in a culture in which everything hinges on money. . . . Few things about education in Middletown today are more noteworthy than the fact that the entire community treats its teachers casually. The more than 250 persons to whom this weighty responsibility of training the young is entrusted are not the wise, skilled, revered elders of the group. In terms of the concerns and activities that preoccupy the keenest interests of the city's leaders, they are for the most part nonentities.

The salaries mentioned by the Lynds are misleadingly high because purchasing power was going down. Teachers' salaries in 1930 were actually less in real earnings than salaries in 1920 or 1925, and they dipped slightly again by 1937.

One reason for the low salaries was that women were a large part of the teaching force. Men were closer to the taxpaying public than women; through their affiliations with civic clubs, fraternal orders, and chambers of commerce, men had excellent opportunities to win confidence and support of influential citizens. But teaching was characterized as a woman's vocation, and women were not considered in need of high pay. As for the teacher's inconspicuousness, the words of President Herbert Hoover in "A Message to Teachers" speak for themselves: "The public school teacher cannot live apart. He lives among his pupils during school hours and among them and their parents all the time. He is peculiarly a public character under the most searching scrutiny of watchful and critical eyes. [But] how seldom does a teacher figure in a sensational headline in a newspaper! It is truly remarkable, I think, that so vast an army of people—approximately 800,000—so uniformly meets its obligations, so effectively does its job, so decently behaves itself, as to be almost utterly inconspicuous in a sensation-loving country." It did not occur to President Hoover, or to many others, that teachers might enjoy a bit of sensationalism, especially if that meant a few more dollars. Teachers, too, were living in a culture in which everything hinged on money, but they were not getting their share of the cash.

NEA GROWTH

The teachers' major national voice, the National Education Association, grew in the 1920s and 1930s from a

29

small group led by college professors and school superintendents into a large and truly national group with the potential for representing classroom teachers. The rise in membership was spectacular. In 1917 NEA membership was 8,466; by 1927 it had grown to 141,212. By World War II it had topped 200,000. The association grew structurally, too. By 1921 NEA committees and commissions were dealing with sources of revenue; visual education; legislation; foreign relations; salaries, tenure, and pensions; research; elementary education; illiteracy; the reorganization of secondary education; health problems in education; thrift education; racial well-being; rural education; elementary school English; high school libraries; and standardization of schoolhouse planning and construction. Departments of the association by 1921 included business education, child hygiene, classroom teachers, deans of women, educational publications, elementary education, elementary school principals, higher education, immigrant education, kindergarten education, library, music education, normal school, physical education, school administration, school patrons, science instruction, secondary education, superintendents, vocational education and practical arts, and wider use of schoolhouses. The association also had obtained permanent headquarters in Washington, D.C., and had employed a staff of about 50. NEA-affiliated associations were based in every state, as well as in the District of Columbia and the Territory of Hawaii. And more than 500 local affiliates were already part of the structure by 1921.

During the 1920s and 1930s NEA also went through two democratizing moves. One brought classroom teachers into full membership; the other set up a Representative Assembly of delegates to establish association policy, with delegates representing every state. By 1925 the classroom teacher had been made a first-class NEA citizen. A Cincinnati delegate to the 1925 Representative Assembly expressed it in these words: "No longer than ten years ago, it was an unheard of thing to ask the classroom teacher to speak in a general session of the National

Education Association, such as this. We came, we sat, and we were conquered. We sponged up all sorts of pedagogic wisdom handed down to us by able administrators who like to talk; and, we must admit, they talked well. Today we are not merely listeners, we are speaking for ourselves." The democratizing changes allowed state and local affiliates to send delegates in proportion to the number of their members. This move, and a further move to cut back on ex officio members of the assembly, led to much wider participation of grassroots members. Some objected to both democratizing moves, even to the idea of expanding membership at all, but NEA Executive Secretary Crabtree and other progressive leaders prevailed, and membership continued to climb.

Although the 1920s and 1930s were times of growth and democratization for NEA, however, they were not times of great militance. Discussion of matters affecting welfare of members occupied only 2 percent of the addresses given at general sessions of the association from 1918 through 1928. In eight of these years, no discussion of welfare took place at all. In 1928 an observer said, "The association certainly cannot be called a militant or 'fighting' group. The tone of its pronouncements is mild and conciliatory, in the main." So, despite the urging of some leaders, NEA's emphasis during the 1920s and 1930s was mainly on membership growth and expansion of services such as publications, research, and federal legislative lobbying. The mechanisms for militant improvement of teacher welfare had not yet been developed and implemented.

GROWTH IN THE STATES

In the state teachers groups, the classroom teacher began to assert himself, too. By 1922 the teachers of each state had some sort of general organization, with more than half of the states holding an annual meeting. But in the country at large, attendance at these meetings probably did not exceed one-third the total number of teaching positions. Teachers were

31

still basically unorganized and had little day-by-day cooperation; what little cooperation there was cropped up during the
days of the annual conference and rarely extended throughout
the year. Classroom teachers were mostly ignored, or ignored
themselves by lack of assertion. In the late 1920s and especially
in the 1930s, however, change and democratization began to
take place. The state groups, like NEA, were beginning a period
of immense opportunity. The Depression was threatening
salaries, and teachers throughout the nation were beginning to
recognize the benefits of standing together against the forces of
society that were ready to deny them their meager salaries. In
state after state, as legislatures and communities cut back
school funds, association leaders found themselves thrust forward as champions of underpaid, sometimes unpaid, teachers.

In this framework of crisis, the classroom teacher fought to
have his (more often her) voice heard. One such struggle is told
by Ruth Everett, a classroom teacher who became involved in
the work of the North Carolina Education Association during
the 1920s and 1930s. Even as membership increased in the
group, she found that control remained in the hands of a small
inner circle which was "not the Board of Directors as elected by
the membership, but a sort of 'kitchen cabinet' to the executive
secretary. . . . The control of the policies and the growth of the
association was directed by a small group of 'political dema-
gogues,' 'book men,' and representatives of vested interest."
Nor did she find recruitment voluntary:

> It was the first teachers' meeting of the year and after a long series
> of announcements, regulations, and suggestions had been made by
> my dear old superintendent, Mr. P. J. Long, we were aroused from
> our complacency by these words from our respected superintend-
> ent: "Fellow teachers, the time has now come to join the North
> Carolina Education Association. I purposely want to make this a
> 100 percent unit. It will cost you $2. If you have $2 in your pockets,
> sign your name on the membership card and turn in your money. If
> you don't have $2, sign a post-dated check which you will find
> among the NCEA materials given you. It is a worthy organization,
> and the magazine alone is worth $2."

32

They all joined, she said. Then the superintendent proceeded to nominate a president and a secretary of the local association, both duly elected. "The year rolls on; each month the magazine comes; each day it is put away with other magazines to be read after one retires for the evening; month by month it comes; but is never read; the superintendent calls other meetings; he presides, announces, regulates. . . . The year is a happy one. . . . We know not that out in the big world there is a professional organization for teachers. The NCEA means nothing to us."

Mrs. Everett was distressed by the superintendent's power in an adolescent organization:

> The situation which existed in North Carolina in regard to democratic organization of professional educational organizations was no different from any other state where professional organizations for teachers were growing up. They "grew down" from the top instead of "up," and they were managed by the executive secretaries and superintendents in every state. That these organizations were managed dictatorially, no one can deny. But with the poorly prepared teachers we had even in 1926, and the lack of professional pride manifested on every hand, we have had these old-time secretaries and administrators to thank for initiating a professional organization movement at all. Colleges and universities had done nothing to instill an interest on the part of the teachers in their professional organization, and it's little wonder that luke-warmness existed when the $2 membership was presented at the first teachers' meeting.

Mrs. Everett related the early attempt by a woman president of NCEA to encourage district meetings in the state and to set up local units. Progress seemed slow, and organizing of local units was still in the future. But suddenly a challenge faced the North Carolina association: The American Federation of Teachers began organizing local teachers. The "powers," frantically searching for some countermovement, hastily organized a Department of Classroom Teachers. One of the demands of the classroom teachers was that a field worker be

33

supplied for the department. Mrs. Everett was named to that post, and she worked to build county and local units of teachers throughout the state.

Although some democratization was under way in some states throughout the 1920s and 1930s, most state associations continued to shy away from militancy or anything that smacked of unionism. Association leaders still believed that the use of coercion by unions was contrary to the accepted methods of education: argument, persuasion, demonstration. "The use of coercion in any way at any time is of itself a confession of failure of educational measures," a Pennsylvania leader said. "Use of any coercive measure is contrary to the basic principles of voluntary teachers association." In 1936 the executive secretary of the Washington Education Association summarized his idea of the proper attitude for an association member. The member, he said, has faith in these means: democracy, unselfishness, cooperation, technology, fact finding, discussion, ethics, professional progress, leadership and followership, and finally, salesmanship.

Union Decline

Nor, with a few exceptions, were teachers to find militant support among their unions during the 1920s. Unions were experiencing a period of decline and disintegration, with some 80 percent of the charters issued by the American Federation of Teachers inoperative by 1928. The rapid growth of the union movement had alarmed school boards and other anti-union forces. Anti-union editorials blossomed in the press; hostile school board members went on the national lecture circuit to warn of the danger of unionism for teachers. By the end of the twenties, AFT membership had dropped to fewer than 5,000—about half the 1920 figure.

The union tried to emphasize salary, tenure, and the social issues which had first given it life, but it had to spend most of the decade just fighting to stay alive. A few strong, well-organized, big city locals in New York, Chicago, Atlanta, San Francisco, and elsewhere survived to provide some leadership during the coming crises of depression and war. And indeed the fortunes of the American Federation of Teachers did begin to change in the 1930s. As the impact of the depression brought more teachers face to face with economic distress, more of them "went union." AFT focused on what it called "the struggle for academic freedom." This struggle, combined with efforts to improve teacher tenure laws and mixed with the generally bleak economic conditions, again gave the union a growing membership—32,000 by 1939. And except for an unfortunate problem during the late 1930s and early 1940s, the union probably would have grown even more. This problem was Communist infiltration and domination of some union locals. During debate about such infiltration, the 1935 AFT convention heard calls for revocation of the charter of Local 5, the Teachers Union of the City of New York. Some years later, the charters of Local 5 and two other locals were withdrawn by a convention vote of 11,000 to 8,000. Thus, when World War II began, the union was torn by an issue that was to cripple it for years. Having drawn members from the most liberal of teachers, it was caught up in the ideological struggles of the left. The union would recover, however; its best years were yet to come.

5 / Low Pay and

Growing Militancy

"Teachers all over the United States are thinking about striking," progressive education leader George S. Counts told a Phi Delta Kappa seminar in 1947. He was not exaggerating. More than 100 strike threats were carried out from 1942 through 1959. These strikes involved more than 20,000 teachers. Further, the strikes were carried out by three types of teacher groups: those affiliated with labor, those affiliated with NEA and state associations, and those independent of both. They occurred across the nation, in large and small districts, but mainly for one purpose: to obtain more money.

In 1946, for example, union teachers in Minneapolis struck because the school board negotiated, they said, in bad faith. The board, fiscally dependent upon other community agencies, was unable to provide the pay increases it promised. The same year, 70 percent of the Pawtucket, Rhode Island, teachers went on strike to demand higher salaries. The chairman of the school board, refusing to bargain with the union while the strike threat continued, ordered a lockout. After two days, the schools reopened when state officials pressured the city to give the teachers a $300 raise. In 1947, when the 2,400 teachers in Buffalo, New York, struck, it was the largest number of teachers to walk out in the history of the United States to that time. The issue again was wages, and after union truck drivers refused to deliver food to the schools, the city had to order all of them closed. The strike caught the attention of the public—and the politicians. Soon after, the New York state legislature enacted the Condon-Wadlin Law outlawing the right to strike by public employees. On January 1, 1949, Minneapolis teachers were told they would work four fewer weeks during the school year and take a 10 percent salary cut. The teachers union closed the schools on February 23. By the end of March, the pay cut was rescinded and the minimum salary was raised. In addition, a $200 salary increase was promised for the coming year.

In 1950 and 1951, New York City teachers conducted a "selective strike," refusing to take part in such after-school activities as coaching sports and chaperoning school dances. By April, 1950, more than 40 high school faculties in the city were refusing all extracurricular activities until a cost-of-living increase was granted. A special investigating committee recommended salary increases ranging from $350 to $1,025 annually, but the raises were not paid, and in May, 1951, the State Department of Education issued a ruling giving the city's board of education the power to compel teachers to resume extracurricular activities. The power was not used, though, and during the summer of 1951 additional pay increases were granted. Only the passage of the Condon-Wadlin Law had prevented a full strike.

In October, 1956, teachers of Rutherford County, Tennessee, struck, demanding a 10 percent increase from the county court, which had fiscal authority. The teachers did not receive the full 10 percent increase but accepted a compromise figure and went back to the classrooms. Earlier that year, the entire staff of the Avoca, Pennsylvania, school system—23 teachers— went on strike, demanding 3½ months' salary not yet paid to them. The school board borrowed money from a local bank, paid one month's salary, promised to meet the remaining payroll soon, and ended the one-day walkout.

These strikes, typical during this postwar period, reflected mostly teachers' anger about inflation. But some of the strikes had other goals which, while secondary to salary gains, were becoming important: recognition of teacher groups as bargaining agents, stronger school personnel policies, and bigger school budgets.

The Norwalk, Connecticut, strike in 1946 is the first example in the nation's history of a teacher group walking out to achieve bargaining recognition. Teachers there refused to sign their contracts and stayed out of school until the board of education granted a salary increase and signed an agreement recognizing the Norwalk Teachers Association as the sole bargaining agent for its members. Nine years later, the Norwalk teachers set another precedent when they negotiated a new agreement that provided an appeal procedure with the state commissioner of education as mediator. It was the first teacher bargaining agreement to provide appeal provisions.

Strikes to protest personnel practices during this period included one in Irving, Texas, in 1955. Teachers and principals walked off their jobs to emphasize their demand for rehiring of the superintendent, who had been fired by the school board. The board responded by firing the strikers. The strike continued until the voters of the district abolished the school district, set up a new one, and rehired the superintendent. In Bethpage, New York, in 1957, teachers walked out to protest the denying of tenure to a principal of a junior-senior high school. Teachers who signed a petition complaining about the denial of tenure were then told they would, in turn, lose their tenure. Sixteen more teachers were suspended for protesting the denial of tenure to those who signed the petitions. After the crisis ended with the teachers' reinstatement, an NEA investigative report said that written personnel policies and proper channels of communication could have prevented the crisis.

A union-organized strike in St. Paul, Minnesota, was called

to force added funds into the school budget. The strike, lasting from November 25 through December 30, 1946, was the most dramatic phase of a long fight by the teachers and an alliance of labor and citizen groups to strengthen the fiscally dependent school board and to get voters to approve more money for the schools. Not until October, 1950 did the campaign make a substantial breakthrough, when the school board was given new powers and the per capita funding limit for schools was increased from $16 to $24.

Post-War Problems

These strikes now seem inevitable in light of the pathetically low salaries at the time. World War II had brought inflation, and as usual educators' pay had not kept up. Further, teacher turnover was high, the shortage of teachers was setting records, and the number of emergency teaching certificates issued hit record highs. Twenty-six of the 48 states were employing teachers at less than $600 per year. Only two states and the District of Columbia did not have teachers earning less than $1,200 a year. The purchasing power of teachers dropped, too, from more than $1,400 a year in 1940 to less than $1,300 in 1943. At the same time, to further aggravate the situation, the purchasing power of factory workers went from about where the teachers' was in 1940 to nearly $1,700 in 1943. In 1942–43 teacher turnover exceeded 35 percent in 10 states; it ran between 25 and 35 percent in 17 others. By October, 1946, NEA declared the shortage of teachers "universal." Emergency certificates, granted to 10,000 teachers in 1940–41, were given to 40,000 in the 1942–43 school year; by the 1945–46 year 110,000 emergency certificates were issued. The crisis was heightened because fewer college students were electing to enter the teaching profession. In 1945 only 7 percent of the college population was enrolled in teachers colleges as compared to 16 percent in 1930.

The pinch between relatively low and static salaries on the

one hand and rising living costs on the other had a "devastating effect upon teaching," NEA said in 1943. Thousands left the profession for higher-paying jobs in industry; thousands of others saw former students, scarcely out of high school, making better wages than teachers with long experience. NEA said that teachers did not deplore the advances made by other groups, but that the public should consider its employees in relation to certain economic realities: "The paycheck of the average factory worker is today at least 80 percent above the year 1939. Workers in shipyards have doubled their earnings since the last prewar year. The net income of farmers will be this year nearly three times larger than the prewar figure. Meanwhile, up to the present school year, teachers' salaries increased an average of about 10 percent."

By 1947 some progress was visible. Several states had adopted minimum salary laws. NEA proposed a minimum standard of $2,400 in 1946; by October, 1947 four states and the territories of Alaska and Hawaii had adopted minimums at or above that. Six other states had passed laws requiring minimums of $2,000 or more. Nevertheless, the average teacher's salary in 1947 was only about $2,380.

In the 1950s salaries continued to climb slowly, but not enough to make teaching competitive with other jobs. In 1951, for example, teachers were actually lower on the economic ladder than they had been before the war. In 1939, the average teacher was earning 12 percent more than the average American worker ($1,420 versus $1,269). In February, 1951 teachers' salaries averaged $3,080, or 4 percent less than the $3,200 earned by the average worker. By the 1958–59 school year, teachers' salaries had finally made substantial progress toward matching other salaries in the nation. The teacher's pay was now above all employed persons and would remain above; the average increase in one year (from 1957–58 to 1958–59) was 10.5 percent; the average pay stood at $5,313.

Thus, just as had happened after 1918, teachers were among the last to overcome the effects of post-World War II inflation. Many left the profession, and of those remaining, Marshall McLuhan (in *The Mechanical Bride*, 1951) could say with some justification, "The teacher in America is admittedly in a peculiar position. Educationally qualified to advance himself economically, he or she appears to take a vow of poverty instead. The judgment of the community on the teacher has long been: 'He can't take it.' Assuming a voluntary noncompetitive poverty, the teacher stands as a reproach to the rest of the community engaged in the scramble for monetary reward. He asserts his 'nerve of failure,' the community retaliates with a certain degree of distrust and contempt. Distrust of his motives, contempt for his lowly status, and lack of gumption."

Organizational Problems

If teachers were unhappy about their pay in the 1940s and 1950s, they were unhappy too about their unions and associations. An Oregon superintendent of schools said in 1946 that teacher groups at all levels were so bad they needed to be discarded and replaced with something entirely new.

Educational organizations are neither fish, flesh, or fowl. They claim to work to improve the lot of teachers and yet they admit the managers of schools and school systems to membership and to positions of control. They claim to speak for teachers and yet they do not require their membership to abide by established points of view. They claim to influence local, state, and national legislation, but the long record of their failures to obtain proper legislation to eliminate inequities in the financial support of schools, to improve educational opportunities for youth, or to make major changes in the organization of states into districts refutes this claim.

This criticism hit home. Education associations, after nearly a century of existence, were still relatively weak. The National Education Association, for instance, made a lot of noise about teachers' salaries and the effects of inflation

41

following the war, but most of this was merely noise. In those years the NEA staff was not large enough to offer much direct help to its affiliates. It was not until 1958 that the association hired two salary consultants and began to hold "salary schools" for its local and state affiliates. These efforts were part of the NEA "expanded program" effort tied to a dues increase in 1958.

One of the reasons for NEA's relative inactivity in such areas as fighting for higher teacher pay during this period was the group's conviction that broad federal aid to education was imminent and would solve much of the salary problem. Unfortunately, broad federal aid was not to come during this period, and the many hours devoted to this effort were to show scant immediate reward. Long months and years of lobbying, bill-writing, and propaganda efforts went into NEA's fight for federal aid. Several times the U.S. Senate passed bills, but the House of Representatives never acted. Finally in June, 1956, an NEA-supported school construction bill survived the Rules Committee and went onto the House floor. Opponents of the bill smiled when Rep. Adam Clayton Powell (D-N.Y.) introduced his amendment to prevent school building funds from going to any state that failed to comply with the civil rights decision of the Supreme Court. Many opponents voted for the Powell amendment, knowing that the amendment would end all Southern support for the federal aid bill. The amended bill failed 158 to 262 on July 5. The Russians came unexpectedly to the rescue, in 1957, however, when they sent up their first Sputnik. NEA leaders shifted strategy and said, "Lack of funds is the basic cause of shortage of teachers and facilities for science instruction." NEA then urged that teachers' salaries be increased as the answer to the gap between Soviet and American science and mathematics know-how. Congress failed to accept this reasoning, but it did pass the National Defense Education Act, supplying funds for specific training and for materials in areas of special need. NEA was unhappy with this "categorical aid" approach of Congress and pressed ahead in the next session of Congress for another broad general aid bill. It, too, was doomed to failure.

Although legislative efforts preoccupied NEA during the 1940s and 1950s, the association also moved in other areas. It launched two programs that would be enlarged in the coming years. One was the Teacher Education and Professional Standards (TEPS) movement, which formed the National TEPS Commission to seek better minimum beginning salaries, annual salary increases, maximum class sizes, and effective tenure laws. Through the other new program, NEA began to defend teachers' rights, establishing in 1941 the National Commission for the Defense of Teachers Rights. This commission also examined possible violations of the NEA Code of Ethics. In 1946, for example, following an investigation led by the Defense Commission, NEA expelled from membership its first superintendent of schools, William H. Johnson of Chicago. The commission also made several widespread investigations of school systems, and its recommendations led to improvement of schools in several communities.

Another NEA change was attitudinal—the association modified its ideas on group action by teachers. Though still condemning the strike, NEA issued a policy statement in 1947 urging "professional group action on salary proposals." The days are gone, the statement said, when teachers bargained individually with the superintendent of schools or the board of education for their salaries. What is needed, it said, are local committees that would negotiate for salaries. It was not until 11 years later, however, that the association began to employ experts to prepare teachers for such negotiation, so the suggested mechanism lay fallow in most school districts.

NEA was building a headquarters staff and an organization that would be a foundation for action in coming years. NEA was becoming a many-sided organization with multiple functions, with staff and machinery developed to handle complex tasks. By 1957 it had a staff of about 440 persons working in 13 divisions, 30 departments, and 24 committees and commissions.

Nevertheless, the philosophy of the association as reflected in official statements remained conciliatory. "No one wins a strike," NEA 1947–48 President Pearl A. Wanamaker said. While teachers were being told by the association that higher salaries were needed, they were reminded that "better service must go with higher salaries."

AFT STRUGGLES

During the 1940s and 1950s, the American Federation of Teachers was in no position to play an active role at either the national or state level. Its national organization was almost nonexistent. From its Chicago headquarters the union made few efforts to influence federal legislation. State teacher unions or state branches of the national union were absent. AFT remained a loose organization of a few strong local unions, notably in Chicago and New York, and a growing number of independent unions, mainly in small cities. At the beginning of World War II, AFT had 13 chartered locals; by 1947 it had 86. These locals were in 24 of the 25 largest cities and in two-thirds of the cities of more than 100,000 population. The number of locals continued to increase from 1948 through 1959, except for temporary losses. Overall membership in the union grew from 37,000 at the end of World War II to 42,000 by 1947, and in 1959 totaled 54,817. (AFT temporarily lost about 25 percent of its membership when it expelled a number of locals which failed to desegregate after the 1954 Supreme Court ruling.) In 1959 the union's total membership made up just 3.8 percent of the public school instructional staff in the nation.

AFT policy during this period rejected strikes by teachers. The union adopted this policy in 1947 and reiterated it in 1951, saying: "The use of the strike is rejected as an instrument of policy of the American Federation of Teachers. The Executive Council and its national officers will not call a strike either nationally or in any local area or jurisdiction, nor in any way advise a local to strike. The funds and facilities of the national organization will not be used to support strikes." The policy statement made it clear, though, that no local would be expelled for striking and that certain services from the national union were available to help with negotiation and mediation. This help was given to a number of AFT locals, some of them in suburbs and small cities. But it was in the big cities, especially New York City, that AFT's future strength would develop.

6 / New York City:

Union Victory

I N THE 1960s the rival American Federation of Teachers and National Education Association met on a common battle-ground—New York City, with its more than 50,000 teachers. AFT initiated the battle. Its local, the United Federation of Teachers, saw an opportunity for a sensational increase in membership. It moved quickly and effectively, easily outmaneu-vering the weak nonunion teacher groups in New York City.

Neither NEA nor the New York State Teachers Associa-tion had attracted large numbers of members in the city. An NEA official admitted, "Perhaps it would be fairer to say neither ever developed the kind of meaningful program that would attract and hold considerable numbers of teachers as members in New York City." NEA, which once had more than 10,000 members in the city, enrolled only 700 in 1960. Further, New York City's professional staff was split among at least 20 groups, divided both by level and role (elementary teacher, high school teacher, high school principal) and by tradition (the Teachers Guild and the High School Teachers Association, both long in existence, for example, lost members of UFT).

New York City had a climate favorable to union labor; UFT obtained promises of support from local labor leaders and from the Industrial Union Department (IUD) of the AFL-CIO, which was beginning to see the unionization of teachers as a good way to open the door to wider unionization of all white-collar workers.

Back in 1958, five of the New York City teachers groups had come together as the NEA Council. Two years later council leaders, along with representatives from four other teacher groups, asked NEA officials in Washington for help in developing collective bargaining. Sensing that the AFL-CIO's IUD might finance an attempt to organize New York City teachers, NEA agreed to establish a regional office there September 1, 1960, and sent along an assistant director of its membership division with instructions to concentrate on service to city teachers. Before NEA had time to reorganize the city's teachers, however, the union played its first ace. UFT called a strike on November 7, 1960. The strike, the union said, would win for teachers the right to bargain collectively. About 5,000 teachers stayed off the job for one day, and the union claimed it had won agreement from the board of education that an election would be held to choose a bargaining agent. On December 30, 1960, the board promised to call a bargaining election for April 1, 1961. But apparently the board had no intention of doing so; instead it appointed a committee to study "If collective bargaining is to be instituted for professional persons in the school system, what would be its most appropriate form?" At public hearings held by the committee, the NEA-affiliated groups opposed the idea of collective bargaining, while UFT spoke out strongly for it. In May, 1961, the committee issued a report calling for a referendum by city teachers to see if they wanted collective bargaining. In that referendum in June, the vote was 26,983 for bargaining and 8,871 against. The referendum also showed that the city's teachers wanted a single bargaining agent, not two or three agents as NEA officials had hoped.

47

When teachers returned to school in the fall of 1961, both groups began to gird for the inevitable battle. UFT had the advantage and never lost it. It maintained unity throughout the campaign; it received at least $100,000 in direct aid and loans from other unions, especially from the Industrial Union Department of the AFL-CIO. On the other hand, NEA had no base to build on. To establish one, it combined the groups that had come to it a year earlier asking for assistance into a coalition of forces for collective bargaining. Called the Teachers Bargaining Organization (TBO) of New York City, the coalition set as its first priority a new salary plan which provided a differential raise wanted by secondary teachers, but included an option allowing some elementary teachers to obtain the same raise. The TBO announced a few weeks later that it had established a bargaining committee in anticipation of winning the election.

The union, meanwhile, concentrated on improving its already favorable odds. It got supervisors and nonsupervisory personnel thought to be leaning to NEA removed from the eligible voting group. It harassed and hampered Teachers Bargaining Organization personnel; in some cases, TBO people were unable even to enter school buildings or to circulate materials.

A ROUGH CAMPAIGN

The campaign was more rough-and-tumble than NEA was used to. As one NEA staff man, T. M. Stinnett, put it:

To be starkly frank about it, NEA staff members came up against tactics which in their relatively cloistered world they had never encountered before. After it was all over, they discovered that copies of every bit of correspondence from the NEA office reached the UFT headquarters before being received by the addressee. Mimeographed materials from the NEA office, processed by trade-union members, reached the UFT office before NEA personnel saw them. Members of the NEA task force scheduled to speak

48

at one of the city schools often were notified by telephone that their schedules had been changed only to find when they showed up that school was out and teachers had long since departed for home, or the addresses given them were not schools but vacant lots. One UFT advocate reported that he dropped by the NEA office one day to check on some NEA research data. He went from the NEA office to the UFT office and was questioned about his loyalty. Word of his visit to the NEA office had been reported by an office worker to the union before he could reach the UFT office.

One of the ironies of the election developed because neither AFT nor UFT had a research staff. Often during the campaign, salary statistics used by union workers came from the NEA Research Division; in at least one case, the NEA materials were merely ordered by mail—and were sent.

Three organizations qualified for the ballot in December, 1961; the United Federation of Teachers, NEA's Teachers Bargaining Organization, and an independent Teachers Union. UFT received twice as many votes as did the TBO—20,045 to the NEA group's 9,770. (The Teachers Union got 2,575 votes.) UFT had won decisively and would from this time represent all of the city's teachers.

UFT TRIUMPH

The union victory in New York City was probably the biggest single success in the history of teacher organizing in the United States. A lifesaver for the national union, the victory brought a huge increase in AFT membership, which stood at just 60,715 in the entire nation in 1961. It also spurred teachers unions in California, Colorado, Minneapolis, Chicago, and Detroit to new efforts. The victory also guaranteed continued financial support for the union from the IUD. It seemed to demonstrate to the nation that teachers were ready to "go union"—and if they did, union thinking went, could other white-collar workers be far behind?

NEA stated after the election that the outcome "will

strengthen the determination of the more than 1,300,000 members of the 7,500 local and state affiliates of the National Education Association throughout the nation. They will increase their efforts to demonstrate that American youth, American society as a whole, and the teaching profession itself will best be served by maintaining strong, independent, professional organization." The major change in NEA's efforts after the election was expansion of its unit working directly on the problems of combating teachers unions in the large urban areas. NEA and its affiliated state associations had long neglected the large cities, which was one of the reasons that NEA and New York State Teachers Association membership was so low in New York City even before the 1961 election. The NEA urban unit, originally called the Urban Project, had been mandated by the NEA Representative Assembly in June, 1961, before the New York City election. At that assembly, NEA members voted to "direct the officers and directors to intensify efforts and to initiate specific action in crucial areas." During debate on the resolution, a delegate made this point: "If we do not take immediate steps to strengthen our local professional organizations, so that they may better render services to teachers and thereby benefit children in those areas, *other groups with nonprofessional objectives will organize these teachers.*"

The union victory did not end the New York story, however. That city would remain a major teachers' battleground well into the 1970s.

In 1962 the United Federation of Teachers called a strike. An almost totally unnecessary act that brought a tirade of editorial blasts at teacher unionism, the strike lasted one day—April 11. At least 20,000 teachers failed to show for work. At issue was a snag in a promised salary increase, with the money tied up between the city's Democratic mayor and the state's Republican governor, each blaming the other for holding up the school funds. The day following the strike, the mayor and the governor met with union officials and "found" the needed money in 3½ hours. The teachers had won a salary increase, but they did not actually receive the increase for six months, because the union refused to sign a no-strike agreement to go along with the raise. The strike itself was illegal, a violation of the state's Condon-Wadlin Law. The city school board agreed not to punish the teachers, however, if they would return to the classrooms.

Newspaper editorial opinion about the New York City 1962 strike was highly critical. The strike was labeled "not in the public interest," "irresponsible," "shocking," "a bitter blow against the city's million schoolchildren," and "a disgrace." Typical was this comment by the *Washington Post*: "The teachers' strike which began in New York yesterday is a tragedy for the whole city—for its citizens whose irresponsible lethargy is one of the causes of the strike, for the teachers themselves whose action, born of desperation, mars the high pretensions of their calling, and for the children, of course, who are the helpless victims of this undisciplined adult strike."

NEA, too, attacked the strike. Despite losing the 1961 election by a two-to-one margin, NEA continued to operate in New York City. The New York NEA office helped form a City Teachers Association. Soon after the April strike, this group called for arbitration of the salary dispute, saying "We believe that teachers should be led *only* by teachers and should not be the pawns of labor leaders." At the same time, NEA denounced the strike as "the disaster that overtook the school teachers of New York." An NEA spokesman went on: "It matters not that after all the fury and turmoil the New York teachers are going to have a few more dollars on their checks in the months to come, as they would have if there had been no strike. . . . What does matter is that for a long time to come, in the New York area at least, school teachers have lost status in the community. . . . With or without the strike there would have been an adjustment of the grievances of the New York teachers. The NEA leadership believes that there is a better way."

New York City teachers did not agree, and more strikes

51

were to come. As the fall of 1963 began, the union said that teachers would not work until a new contract, including higher salaries, was signed. UFT seemed determined to strike, even though the school board lacked additional funds and the state's Condon-Wadlin Law now provided heavier penalties for striking civil employees. Charles Cogen, UFT president, argued publicly that teachers should be allowed to strike. Speaking on a radio show in 1963, he said:

> Why prohibit teachers in public schools from striking while their counterparts in private schools are free to act as they will? It may be argued, on the other hand, that teaching is a sensitive occupation requiring restriction of strike activity. This can hardly be a serious viewpoint in light of the point just made about the inapplicability of antistrike laws to private schools. Moreover, teaching is not an occupation involving the health and the safety of the people as in the case of firemen and policemen. . . . Indeed, under some circumstances the workers have a duty to strike. Such was the case, for example, in the two strikes that the United Federation of Teachers engaged in. Each was called in an effort to overcome the morally unjustifiable failure of the governmental authorities. . . . But aren't the teachers setting a bad example for their students? On the contrary, we are setting a good example. Civic courage and idealism should be practiced by those who teach it. I am confident that our strikes have enhanced the respect which the students have for their teachers.

The 1963 strike threat, in any case, achieved little. Just before the opening of schools in September, the school board produced a small amount of money that meant $32.50 a year more for most teachers and a $580 increase for a few. For publicity purposes, UFT hailed this modest salary raise as a great victory. But Ida Klause, the board's negotiator, said, "It was all done with mirrors."

Again, NEA reaction was harsh. Executive Secretary William G. Carr said the tactics used in New York City before the opening of schools "do not represent values that can be taught to American public school children. . . . [D]eeply disturbing extremes were reached when some of their leaders openly called on all teachers to defy both the statutes and a court injunction." The comment was NEA's last public concern with New York City for years. Although NEA's city affiliate had talked of asking NEA and the state teachers association to take nationwide action unless conditions and salaries improved, and though NEA had considered imposing "sanctions" against the school system, once the strike threat occurred and New York teachers seemed securely lined up behind UFT, NEA dropped the issue.

Within a year, UFT called another strike. More than 11,000 of its members, employed in summer day camps, joined with city recreation workers in 1964 to close the camps. Then, for a few years, UFT consolidated its position as bargaining agent. But in 1967 another, larger strike had New York City teachers again on the pavements. It began as the schools were scheduled to open in September. Summer-long negotiations between UFT and the school board, including attempts at mediation, had brought no agreement. UFT members voted 12,333 to 2,523 to "resign." Picket lines were set up at most schools, effectively closing them. On the surface, the strike was a demand for higher salaries. UFT was asking $7,000 as the starting salary and $14,000 as the maximum salary for experienced, highly qualified teachers. The board of education offered a scale ranging from $6,200 to $12,600 with further increases one year later. When the teachers agreed to return to the schools, their new contract gave them salaries very close to the board's first offers: a range of $6,200 to $10,350 in 1967–68; a range of $6,600 to $11,000 in 1968–69; and a range of $6,750 to $11,150 in 1969–70. But beneath the salary issue lay more subtle issues. UFT was demanding that teachers have the right to remove disruptive children from their classes—a power held by the school principals. Further, the union wanted an extension of its program for educating slum children, a plan it called More Effective Schools. To fulfill these demands would require both the willingness of school authorities to give part of their power to teachers and the willingness of parents to allow a union of teachers to make decisions about what type of education their children would receive. To further complicate the matter, New York City teachers in 1967 included in their number many white and Jewish teachers. To some residents of black and Puerto Rican communities, the teachers' attempts to change school policies (even if for the better) was interpreted as another instance of the white person making decisions for black and brown people.

The strike ended in two weeks. A marathon 26-hour mediation session brought a contract agreement that teachers ratified by a vote of 18,171 to 3,442. Teachers did not win the right to remove disruptive children, but they did get the right to appeal a principal's refusal to remove them. The teachers did not get the overwhelming adoption of the More Effective Schools program that they wanted, but they did win a commitment that the board of education would set aside a fund of $1 million for the 1968–69 school year to develop new programs for elementary schools. Also brought to the surface in the strike was the usefulness of the state's Taylor Law, which took effect on September 1 that year. Successor to the Condon-Wadlin Law, it specifically banned strikes by public employees. Under its provisions, UFT's new president, Albert Shanker, was fined $250 and sentenced to 15 days in jail; UFT itself was fined $150,000. The Taylor Law was passed because the Condon-Wadlin Law had proved ineffective in stopping strikes by public employees. Opponents of the old law argued that its penalties for striking were so severe no public authority would apply them. The new law provided lesser penalties, which theoretically would be more likely to be applied so that strikes by public employees would be lessened. The ability of the Taylor Law to prevent strikes was tested mildly in the 1967 strike, but its true test came a year later when issues of community control, racial composition of schools, teachers' demands, and decentralization combined in school strikes of far greater duration and disruptiveness.

The 1968 Strikes

In a full-page advertisement in the *New York Times* on February 6, 1968, UFT President Albert Shanker said, ". . . we shall not sit idly by while the rights of teachers are trampled. The Executive Board of the UFT is recommending to our membership that whenever a teacher is dismissed or punished without the benefit of impartial review, we will close down the entire school district in which this action has occurred. And we will keep it closed until the injustice has been redressed." Thus the city was warned.

In the fall, Shanker kept his promise. New York City's schools were closed three times in strikes that led to a polarization of social and political groups within the city. Probably the strongest instance of teacher militancy in U.S. history, the 1968 strikes have been described and decried in hundreds of newspaper stories, dozens of magazine articles, and at least five books. Martin Mayer, the author of one of these books, said, "The New York teacher strike of 1968 seems to me the worst disaster my native city has experienced in my lifetime." *Time* said: "Those teachers who crossed the picket lines in an effort to keep some 400 of the city's 900 schools limping along with skeleton staffs ran into a bitter barrage of invective. 'Commies!' 'Fascists!' 'Nazi Lovers!' 'Nigger Lovers!' shouted the highly confused strikers, many of them veterans of years of tortured teaching in the city's ghetto schools. Mayor John Lindsay, wearing a *yarmulke*, was jeered and insulted in a Brooklyn synagogue by a teacher-dominated audience as he tried to explain his stand on the strike. Shanker himself was shouted off the stage at a Manhattan meeting by a highly vocal crowd of black parents, who called him a white racist." The *New York Times* said that the school shutdown "has already aggravated intolerably the worst of the city's racial fears and prejudices. As the strike goes on, the destructive forces of separatism will increasingly contaminate the bloodstream of every sector and institution of this city."

The 1968 strikes eventually involved not only the teachers, but also the school board, the superintendent of schools, the mayor, the state's governor, the state commissioner of education, the state legislature, the city police, and community and parent groups. The focus of the crisis was an experimental school project in the Ocean Hill-Brownsville section of Brooklyn. Ironically, the Ocean Hill-Brownsville Demonstration Project was formed with the backing of the United Federation of Teachers, which saw the project as another way to extend its More Effective Schools program. Residents of the community, mostly black and Puerto Rican, saw the project as a chance for them to exercise a measure of control over the schools their children attended. When the community exercised its control, however, UFT had second thoughts about the project. In May the Ocean Hill-Brownsville project, acting through its administrator, ousted 10 teachers whose teaching was not, in the community's opinion, relevant to the needs of their children. UFT, through Shanker, warned that it would not stand for such actions without benefit of impartial review.

By September 9, when schools were scheduled to open, the ousted teachers had not been reinstated. UFT members went on strike, demanding reinstatement of the teachers, added job protection for all teachers, and smaller class sizes. After two days the teachers agreed to return and the board of education agreed to reinstate the 10 teachers. One day later UFT called a second strike, maintaining that the Ocean Hill-Brownsville project would not honor the agreement and accept the teachers back. The board of education asked the state commissioner of education to intervene. Meanwhile, the city asked the courts to jail Shanker and other union leaders, since strikes by public employees were still illegal under the Taylor Law. The state commissioner ordered the school board to fire the Ocean Hill-Brownsville governing board and to reinstate the 10 teachers. This action did not satisfy UFT, which argued that the community would not allow the teachers to return, and thus the plan was useless. (Earlier, community residents had physically prevented teachers from entering one junior high school.) Instead the union demanded suspension of the experimental project's governing board until the 10 teachers were accepted back, reinstatement of the teachers in the project who had walked out in support of the 10, naming of neutral observers to report harassment of teachers (with the schools being closed in the event of such harassment), and agreement by the board of education and the mayor that they would not approve actions taken against teachers by unofficial groups. As days went by and the schools remained closed, the board of education began giving in to these demands. On September 26 neutral observers were assigned to the Ocean Hill-Brownsville schools; the next day it was announced that police would back up the observers. Negotiations, now involving Mayor Lindsay, continued. The mayor agreed to allow the union to station its own observers in the demonstration project schools.

Schools reopened the last day in September. On October 1, a riot broke out in front of a junior high school in the Ocean Hill-Brownsville project when local residents tried to prevent union teachers from returning to the school. Ten police and dozens of citizens were injured. The school was closed for one day, then reopened. The next week the board of governors of the Ocean Hill-Brownsville district directed the administrator, Rhody McCoy, to remove all UFT teachers from the project's classrooms. At first he refused, but later agreed. The superintendent of schools then suspended McCoy and assigned him to a central school office. McCoy refused to be reassigned. On October 9 another riot broke out at the junior high school, and it was closed again. Meetings of the board of education and the Ocean Hill-Brownsville leaders took place over the weekend, but no effective changes were made.

On Monday, October 14, UFT called a third strike, one which lasted for five weeks. Mayor Lindsay, attempting to settle the strike, closed the junior high school in Ocean Hill-Brownsville that was the site of most of the trouble. The board of education then voted against closing the junior high school, but the mayor closed it anyway. The closing failed to satisfy the union, however, for UFT saw the school closing as a temporary move. Further, under new school decentralization guidelines set by the state legislature, teachers might be transferred to any subsection of the city school district, limited only by the availability of another subsection that would accept the transferee. The state commissioner of education then began working to bring about a compromise. He developed a plan to place the Ocean Hill-Brownsville project directly under state trusteeship. The union rejected this plan as "paper promises," and demanded instead that the state legislature hold a special session to revise its school decentralization plan. The mayor, the superintendent of schools, and others countered by issuing a statement opposing a special session and by endorsing the plan previously offered by the state commissioner.

Other compromise plans were offered and rejected. Finally, on November 17, a "tentative and tenuous" agreement was reached. Two days later, after voting 17,658 to 2,738 to accept the settlement, the teachers went back to work as the city's public schools reopened. The complex settlement was partly what the state commissioner had suggested (a state-appointed trustee to supervise the Ocean Hill-Brownsville project) and partly what the union had wanted (all union teachers returned to the project schools, establishment of a committee responsible for the protection of the rights of teachers and supervisors in all city schools, instruction time added to the school calendar to make up loss in salaries). Even after the settlement, though, the situation in Ocean Hill-Brownsville remained tense. A nervous "cease-fire with intermittent interruptions" continued in the district. In one incident students were arrested during demonstrations at the same junior high school, which was ordered closed. Then Herbert F. Johnson, the state trustee assigned to oversee the district, asked to be relieved of his job. State Education Commissioner James Allen appointed his assistant, William D. Firman. Meanwhile, UFT said it would continue to exercise patience in the face of the guerilla tactics being used by students and others to disrupt classes. A meeting of UFT chapter chairmen urged vigilance to ensure that the strike agreement was not violated.

After the strikes ended, Martin Mayer, who was as close to the actions as anyone not involved in them, gave this summary:

> But there were no real issues in the strikes—just slogans. What is ultimately disgusting about the teacher strikes and the public officials who failed to prevent them is that words like "community control" mean no more in dealing with the complex of relationships between school administrators and the parents than words like "quality education" mean in dealing with the inadequate teacher training and severe multiple deprivation which combine to produce so much wretched work in our slum schools. On words like these, people who knew no better created a confrontation that clawed open the heart of the city. There is no measuring the damage that was done. There is no excusing the leadership cadre who permitted it to be done.

One result of the 1968 strikes was further strengthening of the state's antistrike legislation, the Taylor Law. Its amendment provided stiffer penalties for strikes by public employees by placing strikers on probation for a year, penalizing them two days' pay for every day on strike, and subjecting them to "removal or other disciplinary action provided by law for misconduct." The stronger law also hit at the unions, taking away their automatic dues deduction privileges "for such specified period of time as the Public Employment Relations Board shall determine, or in the discretion of the Board, for an indefinite period of time."

This strengthening of the Taylor Law had little practical effect. The United Federation of Teachers continued to expand its bargaining power. Despite the controversy surrounding the 1968 strikes, UFT came out stronger than ever. It pressed demands not only for teachers' salaries and other benefits, but also for a say in curriculum development and other purely administrative matters. UFT's position became so strong that New York City school administrative leaders feared to make any change, move any teachers, introduce any innovation without bilateral discussions that involved the union. So urgent was UFT's pressure that New York school officials wondered in print if public employers could protect any territory once the collective bargaining process was set in motion—if indeed a public employer was forced to forfeit the responsibility of representing the community. The pressure was reflected, too, among school principals in New York City. Between 1970 and 1972 at least a third of the city's high school principals voluntarily gave up their positions; about 20 percent of the junior high and elementary principals got out. Many of them blamed the school chancellor (the top administrative officer) for not giving them adequate support.

The union continued to ride high. In 1972 it negotiated a contract through September, 1975, covering nearly every nonsupervisory public educator in the city. UFT President Shanker called it "the culmination of our ten-year record as bargaining agent for New York City's public school teachers." The contract, he said, "stands as the finest teacher agreement in the nation." Indeed, the contract was a good one. It provided a top salary of more than $20,000 for teachers with 7½ years service; it locked in tenure; it built in due-process protection of teachers' rights. And it raised higher the star of Albert Shanker.

ALBERT SHANKER

Shanker, a native New Yorker born just before the depression, had climbed into city, then state, and finally national attention. A union worker before he was a teacher, Shanker brought to the union the idea that teachers were part of organized labor, that they should work within the ranks of the AFL-CIO. After helping with the ouster of NEA affiliates from the city, Shanker built UFT into the strongest urban teachers group in the nation. Then, slightly shifting ground in 1972, he maneuvered a merger of the docile NEA state affiliate, the New York State Teachers Association, and his union.

Under the name New York State United Teachers, the new group was 200,000 strong and, uniquely, both an AFL-CIO and an NEA affiliate, with members paying dues to both. Shanker's next step was to take over the American Federation of Teachers, the nationwide union of which UFT was by far the largest local. Smiled upon by AFL-CIO leader George Meany, Shanker won appointment to the AFL-CIO executive council, the only member not already president of his national union. In late 1973 he announced that he would run for AFT president. Using his clout with AFL-CIO and calling in a number of favors from AFT officials, Shanker tried to have the AFT executive committee name him president in December, 1973. But David Selden, the incumbent AFT president, refused to be moved. Shanker's fight for the AFT presidency was part of his "thirst for power," Selden said. The situation also raised questions about a merger between AFT and NEA. Selden had agreed to consider merger outside of the AFL-CIO; Shanker was insisting on AFL-CIO membership. Because NEA's leadership opposed merger under Shanker's conditions, his ascending to AFT power would become a block to merger.

7/ NEA Moves

Toward Unionism

Except in new york city, most teachers in the 1960s and 1970s were NEA members—or members of state and local affiliates of NEA. The associations, though moving with greater deliberation than UFT and AFT, were marching inevitably into teacher unionism. Already in 1960 NEA leaders had okayed a preliminary draft of a statement of principles on what became known as "professional negotiation." Approved by the NEA Executive Committee and Board of Directors during the summer of 1960, the statement called on local boards of education to consult regularly with representatives of the organized teaching profession about salaries and conditions of employment. It urged teacher representatives in such consultations to recognize that boards of education have legal powers and duties in the public interest which they may not with propriety relinquish. It called for voluntary negotiation "necessary to, and fully compatible with, the dignity and ethical standards of the profession." In this mild statement, NEA included a no-strike clause: "In the event of a protracted and serious local failure to agree, the differences must be resolved in a manner that will supply a high quality of educational service without interruption." The modesty of the position is shown by a 1961 NEA Board of Directors statement which said, in part:

Recognizing both the legal authority of boards of education and the educational competencies of the teaching profession, the two groups should view the consideration of matters of mutual concern a joint responsibility. The National Education Association believes, therefore, that professional education associations should be accorded the right, through democratically selected representatives using appropriate professional channels, to participate in the determination of policies of common concern including salary and other conditions for professional service. The seeking of consensus and mutual agreement on a professional basis should preclude the arbitrary exercise of unilateral authority by boards of education and the use of the strike by teachers as a means for enforcing economic demands. Professional procedures should be established which can be utilized when agreement is not reached through joint discussion in a reasonable time, to bring about a resolution of differences.

When this statement was presented to NEA convention delegates in June, 1961, they were told, "One chief difference between this resolution and the 1960 resolution is the elimination of any reference to the term negotiation. This was done not only because boards of education have an aversion to the word, but because under the professional concept, relationships between the teaching profession and boards of education must be profession-oriented, not labor-oriented." The resolution was adopted with an amendment stressing that when impasses occurred between teachers and boards of education, "a board of review consisting of members of professional and lay groups affiliated with education should be used." The addition was urged by delegates from several states who were concerned that labor legislation already in existence in their states might be used to resolve school impasses.

In addition to its abortive role in the New York City struggle and its laying an early, though modest, foundation for teacher bargaining, NEA in the early 1960s continued two programs that boosted growing militancy. It expanded its "salary school," bringing hundreds of educators to its headquarters in Washington, D.C., to learn techniques for winning pay increases. And the association strengthened its efforts to defend teacher rights. In 1961 the NEA Board of Directors approved establishment of a National Commission on Professional Rights and Responsibilities. The new commission took over the work of both the old Defense Commission and the NEA Committee on Tenure and Academic Freedom. This was its assignment:

> Defend members of the teaching profession, schools, and the cause of education against unjust attacks . . . investigate public controversies involving teachers and schools justly, fearlessly, and in the public interest. . . . Encourage the development and use of personnel policies that attract and hold competent professional personnel and prevent unnecessary difficulties. . . . Aid in improvement and extension of state tenure legislation. Promote the civil and human rights of members of the teaching profession and foster conditions of academic freedom under which teachers may safely teach the truth without fear or favor. . . . Gather information about the various individuals and groups who criticize or oppose education. . . . Investigate cases of alleged unethical conduct by members of the teaching profession when requested to do so. . . . Investigate and report to the NEA Executive Committee the name of any member who violates the requirements of Article I of the NEA Bylaws [which spells out qualifications for membership]. . . . Issue reports and engage in such other activities as are appropriate to the development of better understanding by the profession and the public of the areas of concern which are the responsibility of the commission.

With this charge, the commission announced by September, 1961, that it had authorized field studies that could lead to full investigations in five states. Its inquiries were soon to play a larger and larger role in the battles teachers would have with school boards and state politicians.

Meanwhile, NEA expanded its development of professional negotiations—that is, collective bargaining. At their 1961 convention, NEA delegates had passed a resolution dealing with this matter, but not labeling it as such. In 1962 NEA's resolutions committee presented a much stronger proposal. After debate on deleting one paragraph and changing a few words, the delegates overwhelmingly passed a resolution reading:

The teaching profession has the ultimate aim of providing the best possible education for all the people. It is a professional calling and a public trust. Boards of education have the same aim and share this trust. The National Education Association calls upon boards of education in all school districts to recognize their identity of interest with the teaching profession. The National Education Association insists on the right of professional associations, through democratically selected representatives using professional channels, to participate with boards of education in the determination of policies of common concern, including salary and other conditions for professional service. Recognizing both the legal authority of boards of education and the educational competencies of the teaching profession, the two groups should view the consideration of matters of mutual concern as a joint responsibility. The seeking of consensus and mutual agreement on a professional basis should preclude the arbitrary exercise of unilateral authority by boards of education and the use of the strike by teachers. The Association believes that procedures should be established which provide an orderly method for professional education associations and boards of education to reach mutually satisfactory agreements. These procedures should include provisions for appeal through designated educational channels when agreement can not be reached. Under no circumstances should the resolution of differences between professional associations and boards of education be sought through channels set up for handling industrial disputes. The teacher's situation is completely unlike that of an industrial employee. A board of education is not a private employer, and a teacher is not a private employee. Both are public servants. Both are committed to serve the common, indivisible interest of all persons and groups in the community in the best possible education for their children. Teachers and boards of education can perform their indispensable functions only if they act in terms of their identity of purpose in carrying out this commitment. Industrial-disputes conciliation machinery, which assumes a conflict of interest and a diversity of purpose between persons and groups, is not appropriate to professional negotiations in public education. The National Education Association calls upon its members and upon boards of education to seek state legislation and local board action which clearly and firmly establishes these rights for the teaching profession.

This resolution differed critically from earlier NEA statements on negotiation. First, it labeled the process "negotiation" rather than seeking a euphemism. Second, it avoided a total no-strike clause, saying only that "the seeking of consensus and mutual agreement . . . should preclude . . . the use of the strike by teachers." Third, it called for state legislation to require negotiation. Passage of this resolution marked the beginning of a national push for teacher-school board negotiations. It launched an irrepressible movement to formalize procedures for teacher-school board relationships and to legalize these procedures through state laws and school board approvals. NEA's research director, Sam M. Lambert, who later became NEA executive secretary, told the 1962 convention, "Many school boards and superintendents will have to learn new ways of working with teachers associations, and many local teachers will have to learn more effective ways of dealing with school boards and superintendents. The learning process may be painful, but there is no acceptable alternative."

For their part, school boards and superintendents, through their own associations, reacted strongly and negatively to the NEA 1962 resolution. But it seemed inevitably true, in the words of one NEA staff member, that NEA had just begun to "flex our muscles in the effective application of our skills in this area." Before the year was out, NEA's Department of Classroom Teachers held a seminar on professional negotiation at which 44 delegates from all sections of the nation learned how

66

to launch negotiation agreements in their home districts. As part of a general NEA effort to expand the role of the classroom teachers department, the seminar was followed by a series of regional conferences designed to spread the word about negotiation throughout the nation. NEA carried the story of professional negotiation to its membership through its journal, which was sent to every member. NEA also called a meeting of classroom teachers, school administrators, and school board members in November, 1962, in the hope that they might agree on some principles of negotiation. A few agreements were reached, generally saying that written policies and grievance procedures were needed, but full consensus was not attained.

Teacher unions, meanwhile, called NEA's concept of professional negotiation a gimmick and a backdoor approach to negotiations. An unsigned article in a publication of the Industrial Union Division of the AFL-CIO said:

> Examination reveals that "professional" negotiations are a poor substitute for contracts and collective bargaining. They do not terminate in anything so concrete as a written agreement. They amount to a poorly conceived grievance procedure under which assent of the board of education is required to settle the smallest teacher problem. There is no terminal point, such as arbitration. The NEA wants no "labor" conciliators around but believes in mediation by members of a state appeals board with unstated powers. The whole device looks administrator oriented, and a poor substitute for genuine bargaining. It may fool some of the people some of the time.

THE SANCTION

Another mechanism used by NEA in the 1960s was the "sanction"—a kind of blacklisting of school districts. Before 1961, NEA had applied sanctions rarely and the concept was not well developed. But in April, 1962, NEA hired an attorney and assigned him the task of preparing a study on the use of sanctions. It was expected that a report would be ready for the NEA governing bodies within a year, and had nothing interfered, the NEA delegates in 1963 probably would have been asked to vote on the use of sanctions as NEA policy. The normal route was never used, however, for at the 1962 convention a union leader so annoyed the delegates by his challenges that the assembly set aside its rules and passed a resolution on professional sanctions on the spot. The union speaker was James A. Carey, president of the International Union of Electrical, Radio, and Machine Workers, AFL-CIO. He told the delegates that professionalism "is too often used as a substitute for economic dignity." Newspapermen learned that professional titles do not yield salary gains, Carey told them. "Today newspapermen, thanks to their guild, have greater job security than do most of you as teachers," he said. Carey also told them, "There is more and more evidence that teachers cannot afford integrity and honesty." He told them that big business was trying to take over schools and colleges by giving them grants, and he related a story about a Syracuse, New York, teacher who allegedly lost his job because General Electric had ordered him fired. When Carey bragged of the New York City teachers union victory over NEA, many in the audience countered that union money had bought the election. He concluded his speech by saying, "If the charwomen of the schools have sense enough to band together and organize and negotiate contracts, and the teachers do not, I wonder sometimes who should have the degrees."

After Carey's speech, some NEA delegates who were eager to promote the use of sanctions introduced a two-paragraph amendment to a resolution on professional negotiation. The amendment read: "The National Education Association believes that, as a means for preventing unethical or arbitrary policies or practices that have a deleterious effect on the welfare of the schools, professional sanctions should be invoked. These sanctions would provide for appropriate disciplinary action by the organized profession. The National Education Association calls upon its affiliated state associations to cooperate in developing guidelines which would define, organize, and definitely specify procedural steps for involving sanctions by the teaching profession." The amendment was separated from the negotiation resolution through parliamentary procedures; it then passed with little debate as a separate resolution. T. M. Stinnett, an NEA official who was deeply involved in the development of sanctions, admitted later that the resolution would probably have failed without the climate set by Carey's speech. "Only after Carey's explosive speech was it decided to introduce the sanctions proposal from the floor," he said. "The sponsors had correctly gauged the temper of the convention, and the resolution was adopted virtually without dissent. Without Carey's needling, it is doubtful that it would even have been introduced."

Within two months of the passage of the NEA resolution, the Utah Education Association applied sanctions for two days against the Alpine, Utah, school district. The Wisconsin Education Association later in 1962 adopted a sanction policy patterned after the NEA resolution. By the fall of 1962, associations in five states—California, Connecticut, Kansas, Michigan, and Minnesota—had adopted written policies governing application of sanctions. By that time teacher groups in nine other states had taken disciplinary action against school districts, though they had no written policy on sanctions. Those states were Colorado, Idaho, Indiana, Maine, Montana, Ohio, Oregon, Washington, and Wyoming.

NEA Urban Affiliates

Thus, one reaction of NEA and its local and state affiliates to the New York City union takeover was the more rapid development of negotiation mechanisms and of sanctions. Another part of the reaction involved the sudden attention given by the associations to their urban affiliates. Just before the new year of 1962, presidents and executive secretaries of 18 NEA urban locals met in Nashville, Tennessee. Meeting with them were NEA officials in charge of the expanded urban effort. Delegates made a series of demands to prod NEA into greater activity. By March, 1962, NEA had renamed its Urban Project the Urban Services Project and had' appointed Allan M. West, former executive secretary of the Utah Education Association, as director. For the 1962–63 school year NEA budgeted $203,900 for the project, an increase of more than $150,000 over the project's budget the preceding year. By December, 1962, the Urban Services Project, assisted by teams made up of NEA, state, and urban association staff members, had completed evaluation studies of association structure in nine cities. The project also began to publish special materials aimed at teacher-leaders in urban areas. In addition, an Urban Task Force composed of more than a dozen NEA staff members began regular meetings, focusing on strategy as it related to combating teachers unions. Further, NEA spurred its state and urban affiliates to employ fulltime executive secretaries for at least 11 urban units during 1962, bringing the number of such employees to at least 20. The urban areas into which these staff members went included Albuquerque, Kansas City, Palm Beach, Minneapolis, and Salt Lake City.

It was in 1962, too, that a few school boards began to recognize the right of local teacher groups to negotiate for their members. Long Beach, California, teachers, for example, won this right in the fall of 1962. But the negotiation achievement of the year took place in Denver. Despite efforts by the Denver Federation of Teachers and by Colorado Labor Council member Herrick Roth, the Denver Classroom Teachers Association won negotiation rights by a five-to-one vote of the Denver School Board. NEA immediately labeled the decision "significant" and lauded the cooperative method by which it was developed. Denver teachers, with help from NEA, had worked out the agreement with the school board in six months of negotiation. It was the first agreement to offer a large-city NEA affiliate negotiation rights. When Denver's teachers were given a chance to ratify the negotiation contract early in January, 1963, they voted their approval by an overwhelming 2,245 to 357.

Two government officials issued orders in the early 1960s that spurred teacher militancy. Judge Charles C. Stratton of the Los Angeles County Superior Court ruled that teacher groups had the legal right to criticize how schools were run. His decision made it clear that sanctions, applied to force school boards and other officials to change policies, could not be thwarted by injunctions or similar legal moves. On January 17, 1962, President John F. Kennedy issued Executive Order 10988. Titled "Employee-Management Cooperation in the Federal Service," the order says, in part:

Employees of the Federal Government shall have, and shall be protected in the exercise of, the right, freely and without fear of penalty or reprisal, to form, join, and assist any employee organization or to refrain from any such activity. . . . Agencies shall accord informal, formal, or exclusive recognition to employee organizations which request such recognition in conformity with the requirements specified. . . . When an employee organization has been formally recognized, the agency, through appropriate officials, shall consult with such organization from time to time in the formulation and implementation of personnel policies and practices, and matters affecting working conditions that are of concern to its members. . . . Procedures established by an agreement which are otherwise in conformity with this section may include provisions for the arbitration of grievances.

This White House order opened the way for unionization of federal clerks and other employees, to the pleasure of the AFL-CIO. The language of the order, however, sounded more like professional negotiation than collective bargaining, and NEA officials hastened to point out that the term "collective bargaining" was not used in the order. The White House order worked to speed the process of teacher negotiation and/or bargaining. The reasoning went: If federal employees could organize and be recognized, why should state and local employees like teachers refrain?

A TURNING POINT

Thus in the early 1960s the stage for growth of teacher militancy was being set. Teacher leaders of the time could sense the coming changes. NEA Executive Secretary William G. Carr told delegates to the 1962 convention that the association was at a turning point in its history. For the first time, he said, "Forces of significant scope and power are considering measures which could destroy the Association." He defined these forces as "some labor leaders who plan to use their considerable economic and political power to affiliate all public school teachers in a white-collar union—with emphasis at first on the big cities." Such efforts, if successful, he told the delegates, "would redirect not merely the history of the teaching profession, but also the history of free public education. Changes in big cities would soon extend to the smaller places. The loss of contact with the large cities would adversely affect the ability of your state and national associations to serve even in the small towns and rural areas."

NEA was openly admitting that it was in a fight to control the destiny of America's teachers. Somewhat belatedly, and still not fully believing its own words, the association was urging teachers to actions that would, in a few short years, lead to mass resignations, statewide sanctions, and the expenditure of millions of dollars in struggles against recalcitrant school officials. While 1962 was only another year in the gradual progression toward teacher militancy, the year saw a turning point within the NEA establishment. It was in 1962 that all but the most conservative within NEA were forced to realize that teachers wanted more than they were getting and that the unions of the nation would help them get that "more" if NEA did not.

And indeed unions were working to give the teachers more.

The American Federation of Teachers called two strikes in 1963, though neither lasted long. The first strike was called May 2 in Anderson, Indiana, because the school board, AFT said, refused to negotiate with the union's salary committee. After three days, the union accepted a board proposal giving each teacher about $35 in salary beyond the original proposal. About 200 teachers had been involved in the walkout. The second strike occurred May 28, in Gary, Indiana. At issue was a series of misunderstandings between the school board, the superintendent, and the Gary Teachers' Union. Indiana state law at the time barred school boards from entering into collective bargaining agreements, so when the board agreed with the union on a series of matters that added up to collective bargaining, the board president refused to follow through. After the teachers, about 2,000 of them, struck for one day, they were granted the recognition they wanted. The strike probably resulted more from a failure of communication than from substantive issues.

Meanwhile, across the nation, union drives were on to recruit teachers. In 1963, for the first time, the Industrial Union Department (IUD) of the AFL-CIO admitted that it was providing funds and manpower to back the spread of teacher unionism. In October, 1963, an unsigned article in the *IUD Bulletin* said: "Collective bargaining was made possible in New York only because the teachers are part of the labor movement. Behind the determined stand of the United Federation of Teachers was the backing of the city and state AFL-CIO. The IUD has supported the New York Teachers with finances and manpower and now is providing similar aid in teacher organizing across the country." The same issue of the *IUD Bulletin* told of organizing efforts in Los Angeles, Washington, Denver, New Rochelle, and Detroit. A Springfield, Massachusetts, newspaper reported in 1963, "Teachers in this city are joining the teachers' union in greater numbers than ever before." A Hollywood, California, paper reported unionizing attempts in Burbank. And in Philadelphia, as the year neared an end, the

Federation of Teachers prepared for a move to win bargaining rights there. Even in Maine reports reached the newspapers of the distribution of teacher union materials.

The union also turned its eyes toward American teachers overseas, beginning in 1963 a drive throughout Europe to enroll employees in U.S. overseas dependents schools. Further, the union began moving into the college arena, attempting to sign up professors. In addition, union affiliates directly challenged already established NEA affiliates for recognition rights in five teacher elections during 1963. The union won two and lost three of these attempts. The union defeated NEA affiliates in Plainview, New York, and in a contest to represent the teachers of the Milwaukee Vocational School; NEA affiliates won in Meriden, East Hartford, and Wethersfield, Connecticut. These five elections, the first of literally dozens to come, revealed some of the tactics used by union organizers. An NEA staff employee, Arnold W. Erickson, told of three stages in the union efforts in the early 1960s:

First Stage—Drive a wedge between the teacher and his professional association. a) Before they can convince you to like the union idea, they have to get you to dislike the professional association. b) Everything that is wrong with the teaching profession is blamed on the professional association. c) The unions then promise to correct all the ills. Second Stage—Once the union is established, they then seek to consolidate the gains they have made. a) Seek equal rights and status with professional associations. Want to work together. b) Emphasize the democratic principle of all organizations having equal rights. c) Capitalize on the American ideal of giving the "underdog" a break. d) They have an excellent memory as to our code of ethics and will not hesitate to remind us to be nice. (Aside from the union, many of our own members echo the union reminder "to be professional.") Third Stage—After winning the election they now become professional and talk in general terms about improving education. Nothing is critical now, and their statements are hard to attack. a) But they are no longer small, and they work with big labor unions in the city. b) They no longer want equal terms with professional associations. They use

74

union tactics to force nonunion teachers to join the union or leave the system.

The tactics worked to some extent. In addition to winning the Plainview and Milwaukee representation elections, the union was able to record a national membership gain of 10,977 over 1962. It increased its number of locals by 42 and reinstated six additional locals. AFT total membership of 81,798 in 1963 accounted for 4.9 percent of the nation's instructional staff.

During 1963 the American Federation of Teachers also modified its no-strike policy. At their August convention, AFT delegates approved this statement: "RESOLVED, that the AFT recognize the right of locals to strike under certain circumstances, and BE IT FURTHER RESOLVED, that the AFT urge the AFL-CIO and affiliated international unions to support such strikes when they occur."

NEA Reacts

NEA reacted to these union drives by continuing to gird itself for what was becoming a long-range struggle. It added more money to its union-fighting unit, the Urban Services Project, increasing the project's budget to $381,800 in 1963. It had spent $296,787 in the 1962-63 school year. NEA continued membership drives in big cities, resulting in a 7.1 percent one-year gain of urban members by September, 1963. In order to train more leaders to serve its local units, NEA's Salary Consultant Service started regional salary schools to replace the once-a-year sessions in Washington, D.C.

In 1963 the NEA convention again passed a resolution on professional negotiation. Although the resolution was nearly the same as the 1962 one, one key change was made: The more urgent "must" replaced the conditional "should." The revised sentence read, "The Association believes that procedures must be established which provide an orderly method for professional educational associations and boards of education to reach mutually satisfactory agreements."

NEA's Urban Services Project held a pilot seminar on professional negotiation in May, 1963, which involved teams of staff and elected leaders from Newark, New Jersey; Dearborn, Michigan; Denver, Colorado; Champaign, Illinois; Norwalk, Connecticut; and San Diego, California. The NEA Department of Classroom Teachers expanded its promotion of professional negotiation by holding two workshops on the topic during 1963 in Arkansas and Oklahoma. NEA also published its "Guidelines for Professional Negotiation" in 1963. The guidelines, approved by the NEA Board of Directors in June, provided teacher-workers throughout the nation with specific details on ways of becoming a negotiation agent and on ways of conducting negotiations once the right had been won.

NEA's drive to extend professional negotiation was beginning to pay off. By mid-March, 1963, twenty professional negotiation agreements had been won by NEA affiliates in seven states. In October NEA reported that nine negotiation agreements had been signed in the state of Washington. And the negotiation agreement won in Denver late in 1962 brought NEA its first large-city example of extensive salary gains for teachers through professional negotiation. Denver salary raises ranged from $200 to $715 per teacher and pushed Denver's top salary to more than $10,000. An NEA official called the gains "eloquent testimony to the effectiveness of local leadership and to the efficacy of the professional approach to the solution of school problems."

In 1962 NEA convention delegates had suspended the rules and passed a "sanctions" resolution. Part of that resolution called upon NEA affiliates to help in developing guidelines for the use of sanctions. The 1963 resolution, as provided to the delegates by the Resolutions Committee, said that tentative guidelines had been developed and that affiliates should use these guidelines "where appropriate, and through the experience of use continuously . . . improve them." Some delegates to the 1963 convention wanted to go further and include sections from the tentative guidelines in the resolution itself.

The debate that followed revealed that most delegates had not seen the guidelines, and all amendments to the proposed resolution failed. Following the convention, however, the NEA National Commission on Professional Rights and Responsibilities developed the guidelines more fully; with approval of the NEA Board of Directors, the guidelines were published in November. The *Guidelines* stress that sanctions should be applied only:

A. For the long-range improvement of the welfare of pupils, school systems, and members of the teaching profession. B. After a comprehensive and objective investigation under the direction of an official agency. . . . C. When there is evidence that insufficient effort is being made to take corrective action in line with recommendations of the investigation report. D. When the committee investigating a situation where sanctions are likely to be applied is representative of the profession. . . . E. After reasonable efforts at mediation or negotiation have been made and have failed. F. After careful evaluation of the activities and efforts of the local professional association. G. Following a warning that the application of professional sanctions is being considered. This warning will be issued after completion of the investigation hearings, but before action by the NEA Executive Committee, and might be made before completion of the formal report of the investigation. . . . H. By an overall policy-making committee of the association. . . . I. With criteria specified that would be considered in determining when conditions had been improved enough to warrant revoking of sanctions.

The *Guidelines* further recommend that a local affiliate avoid using sanctions on its own, working instead through the NEA state unit. Finally, the *Guidelines* spell out how sanctions may be applied against a school district, school board, or other public agency responsible for the welfare of the schools. Sanctions can be applied, the *Guidelines* say, through:

1. Censure by means of articles in state association magazines, special study reports, newspapers, or other mass media communication announcements or advertising. Reporting of a sanction action

77

does not constitute censure unless the reporting organization is officially a party to the censure action; 2. Notification to the state department of education, and other state agencies, public or private, responsible for or dedicated to the welfare of education; 3. Notification to state and national accrediting agencies of professionally unsatisfactory conditions in a school district; 4. Withholding of placement services, when the state association maintains a placement office; notice to public and private placement agencies of unsatisfactory conditions in a school district and request to observe professional disapproval; 5. Notification to members of an association of unacceptable conditions for employment in such district and the professional significance of accepting or refusing employment in a school district against which sanctions have been invoked; 6. Notification to the National Education Association, and other national organizations concerned, of the invoking of sanctions and the reasons therefore; 7. Seeking state department of education or legal action to compel improvement of conditions, threatening the welfare of the schools or members of the education profession.

Two attempts were made at using sanctions in 1963, but both occurred before the *Guidelines* were available. Both were unusual sanctions. The first was in the form of an "urgent advisory" sent to all NEA local and state affiliates in February, 1963, warning all teachers who were considering positions in the overseas dependents schools that serious educational and salary problems existed in those schools. The advisory resembled a sanction in two ways: it followed a study of conditions in the schools and it publicly notified teachers of those conditions. A second "urgent advisory" was issued November 15, 1963, reiterating the NEA contention that conditions and salaries in the overseas schools were unsatisfactory. In September, 1963, teachers in Waterbury, Connecticut, invoked a sanction of sorts, though they did not actually use the term. Citing conditions as bad in their school district, the teachers refused to volunteer for any extracurricular teaching duties until the conditions were improved. Later in the year Waterbury asked NEA and the Connecticut association to invoke sanctions; the

state association brought the action in November. The Waterbury action bore another similarity to a sanction: It followed an
investigation of the conditions, made in this case by the NEA
Professional Rights and Responsibilities Commission and released in May, 1963.

The groundwork for application of sanctions was also
being laid in Idaho. In April, 1963, an NEA team met with
Idaho Education Association (IEA) officials to discuss corrective strategy after the state's legislature failed to pass a $45
million education budget requested by IEA. In May, 1963, IEA
called for a special session of the Idaho legislature to deal with
school budget problems. No sanction action was taken in Idaho
in 1963, however, partly because Idaho educators were watching
closely a developing crisis in neighboring Utah.

8 / Professional Sanctions:

Power Wasted

From 1955 through 1963, Utah educators, parents, school board members, and other interested citizens joined together to work for improved financing of the state's schools. In 1955 they formed the Utah Coordinating Council of Education, renamed in 1961 the Cooperating Agencies for Public Schools (CAPS). In 1962 CAPS made a comprehensive, statewide survey of Utah taxpayers, which revealed "the almost unanimous agreement" among taxpayers that Utah should increase its school expenditure per pupil to approximate the average of the surrounding mountain states. Following the guidelines of this survey, CAPS agreed on a series of legislative goals for 1963. They were: 1) A per pupil investment in education equal to the mountain states average; 2) conditions of work, including salary, that would ensure an adequate supply of well-qualified teachers; 3) provision of adequate additional services to children, for example, library, counseling and guidance, special education, and vocational education, thus adding more nonteaching personnel to the schools; 4) greater utilization of present staff through an extended school year; 5) provision for full-time kindergartens;

6) elimination of half-day or double sessions; 7) state responsibility for school buildings on a continuing as well as an emergency basis; 8) return to a former method of electing school board members; 9) elimination of the costs to school districts of collecting taxes; and 10) earlier remittance of school funds from the state to the local districts.

CAPS had legislation introduced into the Utah legislature in early 1963, embodying the points in these goals. Utah Governor George Clyde had his own version of a school bill introduced, however, and it became clear that the governor planned to veto the CAPS version if it passed. In the end, though, the governor's bill passed. Utah Education Association (UEA) officials countered that it provided "not enough to take us even half the distance from where we were then to the average of the seven surrounding mountain states." The stage was set for confrontation.

The UEA House of Delegates, meeting March 15, approved a series of resolutions. One "resolved that UEA request the National Education Association to inform its members of the Utah situation and to urge them to refrain from seeking employment and entering into verbal or written agreement with a Utah board of education for the 1963–64 school year until such time as the controversy over school finance has been satisfactorily resolved." Another resolved that UEA members show their dissatisfaction with the legislative action by an immediate halt to contract negotiations for the coming school year, with the interruption continuing until the "present financial impasse has been satisfactorily resolved." This resolution was reinforced by another telling individual members of UEA "to refrain from entering into contractual agreements with a board of education outside of the negotiations being carried on by the Association" and resolving, "Members who fail to comply with the decisions made by the Association at the special convention held on March 16 should be referred to the UEA Ethics Committee for study and for appropriate disciplinary action where it is deemed necessary."

81

On March 16, a Saturday, more than 80 percent of the members of the Utah Education Association gathered in a Salt Lake City stadium. By a vote of 7,788 to 189, they approved the House of Delegates recommendation to withhold contracts until UEA won greater concessions for the financing of the schools. On March 25 Governor Clyde vetoed a bill that would have provided funds for schools and other buildings during the coming biennium; the veto made a special session of the legislature necessary if there was to be any state-financed school construction in the coming two years. UEA leaders hoped such a session would give them another chance to offer school financing legislation; but on April 4 the governor said he would not ask for reexamination of school aid at the special session.

On April 19 NEA telegraphed to UEA, commending UEA members for their "professional solidarity in support of their declared objective of more adequate educational services for children." The telegram urged UEA to persist, promised an investigation of the Utah school system by the NEA Professional Rights and Responsibilities Commission, and urged the governor of Utah to reexamine the need for legislation to consider school needs. CAPS leaders met April 30 with Governor Clyde. The meeting, open to the news media, was used by the governor to deliver a lecture on the democratic processes of government. UEA leaders went away "bitterly disappointed with the governor's apparent unwillingness to negotiate a reasonable settlement of the crisis." Teachers had no alternative, the UEA leaders concluded, but to continue the boycott. On May 28 the Utah legislature held a special session, with school financing absent from the agenda. Utah teachers continued to withhold their contracts for the coming school year. In June an NEA investigation committee began its study of the Utah situation.

Delegates to the NEA convention in July, 1963, passed a resolution backing the Utah teachers. When UEA leaders got back from the convention, they found the Utah governor an apparent changed man—eager to meet with them. On July 14, when they met with him, he agreed to set up a committee to study school conditions. UEA leaders agreed in exchange to recommend that Utah teachers sign their contracts for the coming school year, and at a special convention on August 2 and 3, UEA members passed a resolution confirming this action. The resolution declared that "the present impasse be regarded as satisfactorily resolved and that Utah teachers proceed with the negotiations of contracts for the 1963–64 year." The governor's appointment of a study committee was regarded as "a first step toward the resolution of the present impasse." The vote, four to one favoring the resumption of contract negotiations, meant that Utah schools opened on schedule in the fall of 1963.

CRISIS COOLS, THEN HEATS

In October, 1963, the NEA study committee again visited Utah to continue its investigation. The governor's committee presumably was also at work. As 1964 began, the crisis seemed to be cooling down. Teachers were back in school; NEA's committee was preparing its report. In April NEA presented a 104-page document recommending prompt and vast improvements in school conditions in Utah. In part, the report said: "All responsible citizens of Utah should ask themselves whether they are prepared to make a greater investment in the possibility of a progressive future for their state or whether they are willing to allow the state gradually to drop to third- or fourth-class status through neglect of the educational welfare of the children. The ultimate responsibility for the educational program rests upon the people." The NEA report also optimistically commended Utah Governor Clyde for his "recognition of the urgency of this need and his request for an early report from his school study committee." It urged the governor to call another special session of the legislature.

On May 13 the governor's committee released its report. Like the NEA report, it called for more money for the schools.

It noted that the foremost need of the state was for qualified teachers, and it urged more funds for counseling and testing, school psychologists, adequate school books, increased library facilities, and an expanded vocational school program. Conditions seemed bright for resolution of the crisis. Immediately after the committee report was released, however, the governor issued a statement saying that he would not call the legislature into session. He rejected outright the recommendations of his committee, indicating that he would not take action because the report did not substantiate the needs, did not follow the mandate that he had given it, and did not show how the money for the increased school program could be secured without damaging the fiscal structure of the state.

The UEA House of Delegates, called into an emergency session, immediately voted to ask teachers to withhold their contracts for the 1964–65 school year, to ask NEA to apply statewide sanctions, and to declare a two-day "recess" of schools for May 18 and 19. Almost all Utah teachers struck on these two days, with 7,500 meeting on the latter day to ratify the House of Delegates action. Only 355 UEA members voted against withholding contracts for the coming school year. On the same day NEA invoked national sanctions, "requesting members of the teaching profession to refrain from seeking employment or entering into employment agreements with Utah boards of education until the controversy has been satisfactorily resolved." NEA criticized the governor's actions: "Failing to keep faith with the teachers and many other citizens of Utah, the governor rejected the report of his own committee immediately after it had been presented. This last of a series of rejections of earnest efforts to improve conditions in Utah schools has aroused the teachers of the state. They are determined to bring about higher standards of education in Utah and their objectives deserve the support of their colleagues throughout the nation."

The Utah crisis entered a more intense phase during the summer of 1964. UEA leaders decided on a two-pronged

84

strategy geared toward November elections. First, they asked NEA to continue the pressure of national sanctions and publicity. Second, they organized a political action group to attempt to replace politicians who were opposing progressive school financing. UEA carried out the political fight through its Utah Council for the Improvement of Education, and teachers began interviewing candidates for office and circulating their responses. Friendly politicians were endorsed by the council. In the general election in November, 1964, a new governor was elected and a U.S. Senate candidate who had opposed teachers at every turn was defeated. Eleven teachers or former teachers and 30 legislators known to be on the teachers' side were elected, and a past president of the Utah Congress of Parents and Teachers was elected chairman of the state Board of Education. The new governor pledged an additional $3 million for teacher salaries for the remainder of the 1964–65 school year, adding his promise to seek an additional $7.5 million legislative appropriations in each of the ensuing two years for improvement of education. The Utah legislature followed the mandate given it. Early in 1965 it passed even more funds than the governor had promised. On March 15, 1965—300 days after they were invoked—NEA lifted its sanctions from the Utah public schools. NEA President Lois Edinger declared that this professional weapon "has proved to be a valuable method in winning an important battle for better schools."

Oklahoma Sanctions

So pleased was NEA with the success of the Utah sanction effort that it applied statewide sanctions again, just months later, in connection with a crisis that had been building in Oklahoma since 1963. In May of that year Oklahoma's governor had vetoed a school bill that would have raised teachers' salaries an average of about $1,000 during a six-year period. In July, 1963, the state legislature failed to pass bills that would have increased salaries by the fall of 1964. Stymied,

Oklahoma Education Association (OEA) members attacked the problem in a new way: By petition, they got four initiative measures to improve school conditions and teacher salaries on the November, 1964, ballot. On November 3, though, Oklahoma voters defeated all four proposals.

The state association then asked NEA to begin a Professional Rights and Responsibilities Commission investigation of state school conditions. In December, 1964, the governor refused OEA's request for a special session of the legislature and proposed instead a measure that would finance schools through a highway bond issue. The teachers rejected this as "unstable, contingent on too many *ifs*." The NEA commission's report on the Oklahoma schools found "subminimal conditions in the public school system of Oklahoma in almost every area of the school program." The commission, in a statement preliminary to its full report, said the Oklahoma teachers' salaries were at "a noncompetitive minimum" and that there were "gross deficiencies in physical conditions of buildings, maintenance, health and safety standards, textbooks, teaching aids, libraries, special education, counseling, teaching load, and other provisions basic to an effective educational program."

On March 6, 1965, the Oklahoma Education Association imposed statewide sanctions, saying at the same time that it was ready to adopt more severe courses of action or to withdraw sanctions if conditions improved. On March 10 NEA telegraphed its pledge of "every support in changing the indifference of too many Oklahoma citizens." NEA invoked national sanctions May 11. NEA's executive committee, announcing the sanctions, said it considered four factors: 1) The repeated massive efforts of OEA to secure public support for upgrading public education and eliminating present unsatisfactory conditions; 2) the failure of the state's governor to act on the recommendations for educational improvement made by a committee he had appointed; 3) the general failure of the state legislature and of local and state officials responsible for the

86

welfare of the schools to recognize the importance of the recommendations made by the NEA Commission on Professional Rights and Responsibilities; 4) the need to impress upon the citizens of Oklahoma and their officials the fact that public education in their state was far below any acceptable standard. During the summer of 1965, delegates to the NEA annual Representative Assembly voted support for the Oklahoma sanctions and urged "all local and state associations to contribute generously to the Oklahoma Teachers Emergency Fund."

The Oklahoma crisis ended in September, when voters of the state approved a constitutional amendment that made it possible for local school districts to increase school-support levies. Oklahoma Education Association sanctions were withdrawn September 18, NEA sanctions September 24. NEA declared that the Oklahoma action had proved for a second time "that sanctions are a powerful weapon in the professional association arsenal." The executive secretary of NEA's Professional Rights and Responsibilities Commission called sanctions "the mightiest weapon in the arsenal of the teaching profession." But he added a prophetic warning: "They have also become apparent as a dangerous weapon and one that is not as well understood as it should be."

Florida Sanctions

Ignoring this warning, NEA imposed national sanctions upon an entire state again in 1967. An educational crisis had been building in Florida since March, 1965. At that time the Florida Education Association (FEA) had asked the state legislature to take steps to improve school conditions. When the legislature failed to act positively, the association asked NEA to investigate Florida school conditions. The NEA investigation was made by a committee set up by the NEA Professional Rights and Responsibilities Commission. In March, 1966, the committee reported that politics and tax weaknesses were at the heart of the problem. The report was timely because 1966 was a gubernatorial election year in Florida. The winning candidate, Claude A. Kirk, Jr., had said during the campaign that he would "make Florida first in education." In February, 1967, the governor's cabinet recommended, with the governor's approval, a series of school improvements, including more kindergartens, expanded programs for exceptional children, more money for libraries, and additional first-grade teachers. Several months before the recommendations, the Florida Education Association had invoked sanctions in rural Marion County after a team of its investigators had found "deterioration of the school system, made progressively worse by public apathy and inadequate finances."

But politics is not without surprises. In April, 1967, Governor Kirk dramatically reversed himself. In a television appearance he recommended budget cuts in the very areas his cabinet had urged additions. FEA reacted by imposing two sanctions on May 24, then adding three more on June 3. The five FEA sanctions called for 1) censure of the governor for "lack of leadership for a positive school system"; 2) national circulation of notices that Florida schools were not satisfactory for teaching; 3) national notice to business and industry of these conditions; 4) national notice to individuals outside the state that they would be acting unethically to accept teaching positions in the state; and 5) statewide notice that individuals not presently employed in the Florida school system who accepted such employment would be subject to charges of unethical conduct. On June 5 NEA imposed two national sanctions. One censured Governor Kirk and "those legislators who support his program as it applies to the schools"; the other asked educators to refrain from seeking employment in Florida until "the governor and the legislature provide substantial financial support for education."

The intent of the FEA and NEA actions was to influence Florida legislators who were then meeting, and on June 16 the legislators passed a bill appropriating more money for the schools. This action fulfilled the basic requirements of the sanctions statements and should have led to an end of the crisis. Instead, the crisis worsened when Governor Kirk immediately vetoed the bill. The legislature put through a second school bill, this one accommodating the governor by cutting funds in some areas as he had asked. The governor vetoed items from the bill, cutting $150 million from school moneys.

When the NEA Representative Assembly met in early July, 1967, it voted "full support to the Florida Education Association and the NEA executive committee in imposing sanctions on Florida's public schools." Following this mandate, the NEA executive committee stiffened the NEA sanctions July 21, voting to advise immediately the nation's leading corporations, banks, industrial organizations, and the financial press of deficiencies in the Florida public school system. To apply more pressure, 35,000 Florida teachers held a rally in the Tangerine Bowl in Orlando in August, and FEA began collecting signed resignation forms from its teachers. NEA gave FEA $50,000 to finance continued efforts.

When Florida schools opened in September, teachers in Broward County remained out of school for seven days. They returned only after the county school board agreed to recognize their association, to grant higher salaries, and to urge county delegates to the Florida legislature to support convening of a special session "so that the problems of the schools in Broward County, as well as all of Florida, can be resolved immediately." Teachers in Pinellas County delayed the opening of schools for one day to achieve much the same ends. On September 5 Governor Kirk appointed a special study committee to examine state school finances again. FEA sponsored a "crisis Sunday" open house October 1 in all public schools in the state, designed to let the public see how bad school conditions were. FEA also announced a mass meeting for Sunday, October 22, at which members would vote on withdrawing services. But the meeting was never held, for on October 18 FEA and the governor agreed on a plan that promised to end the crisis.

89

NEA President Braulio Alonso reported the action to the press:

Just a short while ago, the Executive Committee of the National Education Association acted to hold in abeyance the national sanctions against the state of Florida. This was done in conjunction with the Florida Education Association, and it came about because of an agreement reached between the Governor of Florida and the Florida Education Association—an agreement in which the Governor has agreed to call for the report of his special committee at a much earlier date (by December of this year) and to call a special session of the legislature by the middle of January, 1968, to consider the problems of Florida schools. Because of the agreement . . . an agreement which is satisfactory to both parties concerned and which will prevent the mass resignation of teachers which was scheduled on Monday . . . the NEA will hold its national sanctions in abeyance.

So again the Florida crisis seemed on its way to resolution. But when the governor's committee turned in its report in December, it was discovered that the report, though containing suggestions for improving Florida public education, did not suggest how funds should be raised for these improvements. Governor Kirk then announced plans to take the matter of a tax increase to the public through a statewide referendum. "Any tax the people want to put on themselves, they're welcome to do," he said.

FEA's delegate assembly met on December 28. Rejecting the governor's idea of a referendum, the delegates voted unanimously to walk out of the classroom March 1 unless the legislature passed laws to provide $400 million for the schools. Some 32,000 resignation forms were filed at FEA headquarters. On January 29 Governor Kirk, addressing a special session of the Florida legislature, reiterated his position that "any increase in taxes or any changes in taxes be tied to public approval of the changes involved in restructuring our system of public education." The legislature went to work. The state senate rapidly approved a $225 million education package of improvements for the public school program from kindergarten through grade 12. Hopes rose. The Florida house refused to accept the senate program, however; it reduced the program by almost $100 million and tied in a provision for property tax relief favoring large landowners and business interests. A compromise bill raised $351 million in new taxes in the name of education, but out of that the K-12 program, where the greatest need lay, was to receive only a little more than a million dollars.

When Governor Kirk threatened to veto even this compromise bill, FEA called on its members to walk out. A total of 26,000 teachers throughout the state did not report to their classrooms Monday, February 19. The next day the state authorized hiring of uncertified substitutes to reopen all schools. Governor Kirk, who was on a speaking tour in California, told the press that the situation "doesn't appear to be that bad." Rather than hurry back to Florida, he would wait to see what happened. What happened was that the number of striking teachers dropped as the walkout continued. In some Florida counties, school boards obtained injunctions requiring that the teachers return. NEA urged that all the schools of the state be closed "to protect the safety and welfare of the schoolchildren." The Southern Association of Colleges and Schools warned that the Florida schools could lose their accreditation because they were employing unqualified teachers. NEA protested to President Lyndon Johnson and to other federal and Florida officials that "several major companies with U.S. Defense contracts, as well as the military, are providing personnel to man the public schools of Florida."

NEA announced March 2 that it was providing $2 million for interest-free loans to Florida teachers, for legal fees, and for grants to teachers who were hardship cases. NEA had already dispatched dozens of staff workers to help FEA officials handle the situation, and staff from several other state associations were also sent in. Declaring "Today it is Florida, tomorrow it may be your state," NEA called on every member in the country to contribute a day's pay to help Florida teachers. NEA

91

also made available its computer-based job locator service to help Florida teachers find jobs outside the state.

FEA and NEA kept as much pressure on as they could. On March 6 the compromise bill passed by the legislature became law when the twenty-day period allowed for a gubernatorial veto passed. With the threat of a veto gone and realizing that "this appears to be all we can reasonably expect to gain for education—at this time—without completely destroying the state's system of public education," FEA decided to end the walkout. All Florida ,teachers were told to return to their classrooms. But before the teachers could return, further complications arose. NEA learned that several county school boards in Florida would not reinstate teachers who had resigned. Administrators and classroom teachers were punished for taking a leadership role in mass resignations. To add to the pressure, NEA continued its national sanctions on the state, declaring, "The sanctions will not be lifted until all of the resigned teachers who wish to return are fully reinstated." Nevertheless, by the end of the spring term of school, only 16 of the 67 counties in Florida had fully reinstated all of their teachers. In early April NEA said that about 500 teachers were still out of school.

In mid-March NEA had dispatched a team of educators throughout the nation to "tell the 'real story' about the Sunshine State's public school crisis." The truth squads, as NEA called them, were expected to explain that "many county school boards, rather than reinstate thousands of Florida's most experienced and dedicated teachers, have chosen to replace them with unqualified substitutes—many paid at twice the rate of regular substitute teachers—and far less experienced substitutes." Some of the truth squads did as expected. But one squad member, on learning that sanctions had been declared in a state near which he was speaking, said, "I feel very sorry for the people who have voted sanctions today on their state. I hope they can get something from us and our state that will head off what we've been through . . . [and] if they cannot head it off, then this is going to wreck their state. We at FEA took a calculated risk. We figured that when we walked out we would close the schools of Florida . . . but we failed to close the schools; public apathy was endemic; people were not informed on what we were doing or why, so they were angry at the teachers for walking out."

Nevertheless, NEA declared, "Florida teachers have won one of the most significant victories in the history of American education." NEA's executive secretary explained, "Because of the courage and determination of Florida teachers, the financial deterioration of the state's schools has been halted. The state legislature has provided $446.2 million in additional funds for education. There has been a 71 percent increase in the state's minimum foundation program for the schools, and average teachers' salaries will go up more than $2,000. I know of no state that has gained as much for education in a single year." Others had different opinions. The American Federation of Teachers called the strike dangerous, saying, "Florida teachers by the thousands are turning to the American Federation of Teachers for aid" after having lost their jobs in Florida. Bitterly, FEA struck back, saying the AFT "has failed miserably in its drive to recruit Florida teachers. . . . The AFT has nothing to offer the teachers of Florida except false claims and empty promises."

A former FEA staff member gave this summary:

Thousands of Florida teachers walked out, certain that a settlement would bring immediate job reinstatement and that the strike would provide impetus for favorable public reaction to teacher demands for improvements in physical plants and student welfare. This happened in a few counties. But as of June 30, sanctions were still in effect in most Florida counties. Hundreds of educators, including principals and supervisors, had been demoted or fired outright. And, while some counties did pass local bond issues for improvements in teacher salaries and institutional benefits, voters in other areas of the state voted *no* mills for public education.

With school opening only a few weeks off, many county school boards in Florida face financial crises and moods of public anger and indifference far worse than existed before Florida's teachers walked out.

James Cass, education editor of *Saturday Review*, reached a similar conclusion: "But when they returned to their classrooms, overwhelmingly they were not only defeated, but disillusioned. No one cares, they said, except us. The state responds only to power, the local school boards are more interested in retaliation than in education, and even the parents remain unconcerned. So why should we continue to care? Perhaps this is the most destructive legacy of all."

Florida teachers had learned that a teacher strike needed a target that was more directly responsible to pressure than a legislature, and one that could make a decision faster.

On August 22 NEA lifted its sanctions against Florida at the request of the Florida Education Association, which had removed its sanctions August 16. NEA said the sanctions had served their purpose, adding, however, that the case was not closed: "NEA will assist FEA and the Florida schools in every possible way as they move ahead with their important task of educating Florida children and youth."

The Florida sanction by NEA, the association's longest involvement in such a statewide action in its history, was probably its last. A few years later, NEA officials made it clear that statewide actions of the Utah, Oklahoma, and Florida type would not be encouraged. The NEA assistant executive secretary who had directed the Florida effort was fired. Florida had taught NEA a lesson: The American public was not so fully on the side of its teachers that it would place their needs first. As a result, NEA turned away from sanctions and strengthened its use of more traditional mechanisms of labor unions: achieving contracts; getting the rights of teachers in writing; striking if necessary, but selectively, district by district. NEA learned, too, that the prestige of the national organization should not be put irreversibly on the line in any single struggle. NEA had learned to fight where it had to and in the way required, knowing now that if it lost one battle, it would survive to fight again.

9 / Teacher Strikes:

Power Demonstrated

S ANCTIONS HAD LED TO A DEAD END—a side trip education associations took down a road that led nowhere. It now seemed no simple ways, no dramatic new mechanisms would resolve teacher-school board or teacher-legislature conflicts. So associations fell back on the traditional labor mechanism—the strike. Of course, throughout the years when sanctions were being applied, many conflicts were being resolved by the strike. At least a dozen teacher strikes took place in school systems in 1964, for example.

JERSEY CITY AND EAST ST. LOUIS

The first strike of the year broke out in Jersey City, New Jersey, when members of the education association called in "sick" on March 4 to protest cuts in the school budget. The association also sued the mayor, members of the two councils, and the board of education for $775,000 in back pay. The teachers went back to their classes after one day, and the suit was dropped after a compromise added $230,000 to the salary pot for the coming year. East St. Louis, Illinois, teachers spent most of 1964 either demonstrating or striking. They struck for four days, starting May 18, demanding a 6 percent pay increase for the coming year. As part of the agreement to return to work, they asked for pay covering the four days of the strike. The school board agreed to extend the school year for four days to provide the extra pay, but a citizens' suit blocked the extension. As a result, the union began demonstrations June 18, 1964, but did not ask teachers to leave their classrooms. During the summer of 1964, the school board agreed to give nonteaching personnel a 10 percent raise; the union in turn demanded that its raise also be increased to 10 percent. Schools were picketed beginning September 1, the first day of school, with 433 of the system's 722 teachers going out. The strike ended when the school board agreed to pay the 10 percent, provided funds could be found.

HOBOKEN AND BAYONNE

Many Hoboken, New Jersey, teachers called in absent for "personal reasons" for one day, June 2, 1964. The teachers, members of the local education association, were seeking a pay increase. The school board, the mayor, and the board of school estimate were involved in a three-way argument about the schools, and the teachers did not get their raise, though the one-day strike ended. An abortive strike took place in Bayonne, New Jersey, on February 8, 1964. Both the federation of teachers and the teachers association had members in the city. The union teachers—52 of them—walked out, expecting the majority affiliated with the professional association to follow. They did not, and a few months later the Bayonne Teachers Association was recognized by the school board as the bargaining agent for the city's teachers. A strike called by the Pawtucket, Rhode Island, School Alliance brought its teachers a salary raise and negotiation rights. The strike began October 5 and lasted until October 14. In all, about 400 of the city's 500-person school staff struck for six working days.

CATOOSA COUNTY AND LOUISVILLE

The South saw teacher strikes during this period, too. Twenty-three of the 29 teachers at Lakeview High School in Catoosa County, Georgia, struck on November 2, 1964, when it became known that there weren't enough funds to pay them for the month of November. After other teachers in the county— members of the Catoosa County Education Association—expressed sympathy with the strike, a citizens' group raised funds for the salaries. In Louisville, Kentucky, a brief strike foreshadowed more serious problems in that state. On November 3, 1964, Louisville area voters rejected the fourth consecutive attempt for approval of a raise in the property tax and for the imposition of other taxes. Without the added funds, the schools were hard pressed to keep going. Following the tax defeat, concerned teachers from the Louisville Education Association and the Kentucky Education Association met to plan a course of action. The associations allowed the president of a small (50-member) teachers' union to speak at the meeting. When the president called for a strike, many teachers cheered. The following day, about 300 teachers stayed out of school, even though the Louisville association had not called a strike. The number of teachers on strike diminished each day, however, and November 15 the union called off the strike. Although little of immediate consequence was accomplished by the strike, it did alert teachers and citizens to school problems in Kentucky and prepared them for a statewide teachers' walkout in 1966.

BELLEVILLE AND PAWTUCKET

Teachers walked out in nine school districts during 1965. Four of the walkouts took place during the spring session of school. The first occurred March 19, when Belleville, New Jersey, teachers staged a one-day walkout in protest of bad school conditions. Later the Belleville schools were the subject of an NEA Professional Rights and Responsibilities study. The study pointed out that teacher turnover was high in Belleville and that the citizens often had rejected ballots to improve school financing. The one-day strike took place after a school budget proposal was defeated February 9, 1965, forcing the town council to cut the school budget. As a result of the strike, the school budget was restored and a day was added to the end of the school year to make up for the strike day. The second teacher strike of 1965 occurred in Pawtucket, Rhode Island, where conditions were about the same as they were during a walkout in 1964. The dispute centered on who controlled the city's schools—the mayor, the school committee, the teachers, or the state. All were involved in the bitter 1965 dispute. The political struggle in Pawtucket had been going on for about 20 years, with members of the Pawtucket Teachers Alliance opposing both the school committee and the strong hand of the mayor and his political machine. When the union and the school committee failed to negotiate successfully early in 1965, the union sent a telegram to the state's governor threatening a strike. A union-school board meeting on February 25 ended in angry words on both sides; a month later the teachers walked out. They returned to school April 7 after a court had cited them for contempt. (The union and its negotiating committee subsequently were found guilty.) The conflict continued, with the school committee unilaterally setting the salary schedule for the coming year and docking teachers' pay for the days of the strike. But in 1966, a contract was achieved, and it included a "no reprisals" clause.

HAMTRAMCK

On the night of April 26, 1965, about 80 percent of Hamtramck, Michigan, teachers literally sat down and refused to teach. Bringing blankets, coffee, and cards into the schools, the teachers began a "sit-in." They remained in the schools until April 29, when the school board agreed to bargain with them. At issue was the board's reluctance to give teachers what they believed was a fair share of the school budget. The Michigan statewide average percent of school budget spent for instruction (mainly teachers' salaries) was 70.1 percent in 1965; Hamtramck spent 64 percent. The strike ended when the school board agreed to increase salaries and to reapportion the budget. The salary and benefit package totaled $139,500, raising instructional spending to 70.2 percent of the budget. The teachers had been organized by the Hamtramck Teachers Federation, which one year later won recognition as sole bargaining agent for the town's teachers.

South Bend

The fourth and final strike of the spring semester of 1965 took place in South Bend, Indiana, where the South Bend Federation of Teachers called on its 350 members (out of 1,350 teachers) to strike. Ostensibly the demand was for a higher salary schedule than the school board offered; the South Bend Education Association had already accepted it. But salaries were not the real issue. The union hoped to get bargaining clout with the school board. When the strike ended six days after it had begun May 11, the matter of salaries was forgotten and the union claimed it had won the right to meet with the board and the school administration. The board had agreed, actually, to meeting with both the association and the union.

Box Elder, New York, Perth Amboy

The opening of the school year in the fall of 1965 was delayed in Box Elder, Utah, by the refusal of teachers there to attend until they got higher salaries and until their right to negotiate was clarified. School had been scheduled to open with a teachers' institute August 26; school finally began September

8, following a compromise on salaries and an agreement on negotiation rights. A wildcat strike by athletic coaches in some of New York City's high schools threatened to delay the extracurricular sports schedule in September, 1965. The United Federation of Teachers declared the strike illegal, and it soon ended. The football season began on schedule October 2. On November 1, 1965, the Perth Amboy (New Jersey) Teachers Union, which had as members about half of the city's 281 teachers, called a strike in an attempt to force the school board to hold an election so teachers could choose a bargaining agent. Although union teachers stayed out for 12 days, most pupils remained in school, and the strike died. A few weeks later the board called a representation election, but the Perth Amboy Education Association went to court and obtained a ruling stating that the board did not have the authority to hold such an election under state labor law. No election was held in 1965.

On November 16, 1965, nursery school teachers in Berkeley, California, began a strike to protest the firing of four teachers, members of Local 1630 of the AFL-CIO Alameda County Federation of Nursery School Teachers. Although the strike was held without consultation with the union, it supported the action, and the strike by about 30 teachers continued into December, when mediation by the Berkeley Human Relations and Welfare Commission brought about a compromise.

Newark

The final teacher strike of 1965 occurred December 2 and 3 in Newark, New Jersey. The Newark Teachers Association had won representation rights that were to run through July, 1966. Negotiations on the coming year's salaries and on working conditions were scheduled to begin December 1, 1965. The Newark Teachers Union voted to strike to prevent the association and the school board from negotiating; the union also wanted an early election to give teachers another chance to choose a new bargaining agent. The school board tried to block the strike with a court injunction, but the union struck anyway, pulling nearly 800 of the system's 3,200 teachers out of classes for two days. Few schools closed down, though, and the strike ended with no change in the school board's position.

In 1966 strikes by teachers burgeoned. "Strikes and threats of strikes by public employees, particularly school teachers, are proving a virulent fever. And the fever spreads," the *Detroit Free Press* said. During the 1950s and the first half of the 1960s, strikes by teachers had never numbered more than 20 a year. In 1966 at least 33 strikes were recorded by the U.S. Department of Labor's Bureau of Labor Statistics; in addition, several major strikes were threatened but not carried out. The strikes and strike threats were called by unions and by associations. At issue in most of them was the right of teacher groups to be recognized as bargaining agent.

PLAINVIEW, NEW ORLEANS, AND YOUNGSTOWN

Typical of these strikes were two in March. About 400 teachers walked out early that month in Plainview, Long Island, New York. The teachers struck on a Tuesday and returned the following Monday after a mediator worked out a 10-point agreement between the union and the school board. Basic to the agreement was a written contract: the board agreed to sit down at the negotiating table with the union. The other March strike occurred in New Orleans, where the teachers union was a minority group. Again, the goal was to force the school board to negotiate with the union, and by doing so win teachers to its side. The strike failed after three days because the union had not laid a solid groundwork; the New Orleans community strongly opposed the strike, even to the point of counter-picketing the union teachers.

Similar to the New Orleans strike was one called in November by a union in Youngstown, Ohio. As in New Orleans, union members were a distinct minority in the school system, numbering about 200 of the approximately 1,250 instructional staff. The Youngstown Education Association, with membership of more than 950 members, had a written negotiations agreement with the board of education because of its clear majority of members. The union struck for a week in November, demanding first an immediate election to determine representation rights and then, when the association agreed to such an election, demanding separate elections for teachers and nonteachers on the staff. The agreement between the association and the school board called for an election in 1968; the association agreed to a compromise under which the votes of teachers and nonteachers would be counted separately, and the union ended its strike. This pattern of strikes to force recognition of a union or an association also cropped up in Michigan in 1966. Strikes throughout the state (as in Highland Park, Crestwood, Flint, Northville, Wayne, and Ecorse) were called to force school boards to negotiate with teachers. This pattern was repeated in Michigan in 1967 and 1968.

A few strikes during 1966 were centered on issues other than recognition of a bargaining agent. For example, Kansas City, Missouri, teachers—both union and association—held a one-day walkout October 3 to protest the board of education's refusal to approve what the teachers thought was an adequate school tax levy proposal. Union members in Richmond, California, struck for seven days to protest the state's Winton Act, which had set up negotiating councils that blocked minority group—usually AFT—representation. And teachers in Decatur, Illinois, walked out for two days in a demand focused on salaries.

Among strike threats not carried out in 1966 were those in Minneapolis and in Baltimore. Teachers in Minneapolis were upset when their state legislature passed a law allowing most public employees—but not teachers—to engage in collective bargaining. Union teachers threatened a strike in March to protest the law. The union's rival, the City of Minneapolis Education Association, said it believed that the best way to clarify bargaining rights was to lobby the legislature, but the Minneapolis Federation of Teachers wanted to strike. Since strikes by public employees were illegal in Minnesota, the city's school board obtained a court order enjoining a walkout, and the strike did not materialize. The Baltimore Teachers Union used the strike threat for a different reason. The union's threat of a walkout in May, 1966, was attributed to a concern for a $4.2 million slash in the school budget and its consequences for teacher salaries. But the threat really served the purpose of drawing attention to a then-minority union. Baltimore had been selected by the American Federation of Teachers as a prime target for union takeover—which actually took place two years later.

College Strikes

Several 1966 strikes occurred in a relatively new setting—the campuses of two- and four-year colleges and universities. The sudden appearance of strikes by college professors reflects the organizing success the American Federation of Teachers was having. In the words of AFT's journal: "1966 may well go down as the year the American college professors made their initial leap from the ivory tower onto the firm ground of trade unionism." The largest of the professors' strikes involved the Chicago junior college system. More than 650 faculty, members of the Cook County Teachers Union, struck to protest the refusal of the junior college board to negotiate with their union. The most dramatic strike of the year occurred at St. John's University in New York City, where 31 professors, 21 of them union members, were dismissed without hearings or notification of the reasons for their dismissal. Union teachers, civil rights workers, persons working for liberalization of the Catholic Church (St. John's is a church-operated college) joined to protest by picketing and debate that continued throughout 1966.

Ironically, in this year of teacher strikes and strike threats, both NEA and AFT spokesmen were speaking against them. Early in 1966 AFT President Charles Cogen, in his monthly column to members, said: "Moreover, short of the strike, we have many tactics that are militant and often effective. These include petitions, strong statements at board meetings and in publicity, demonstrations, rallies, and picketing. These are indeed days of dynamic change in our schools, as well as in society in general. We need not, and should not, go out of our way to look for a fight. Sound militancy is not consonant with irresponsibility. We are and should remain a union of militant professionals."

NEA, speaking out against a union strike in Newark, New Jersey, found itself in an embarrassing position when its own Newark affiliate then went out. NEA's executive secretary, William G. Carr, issued a statement condemning the first strike; "I congratulate the teachers of Newark for standing fast in the face of a disruptive, sore-loser strike effort by union teachers in the city. The walkout is clearly a shoddy effort to disrupt continuing negotiations between the duly elected representative of all the teachers—the Newark Teachers Association—and the Board of Education. In fulfilling your teaching commitment, you are keeping faith with the people of Newark and with the New Jersey Education Association and the NEA, who pledge you their full support. This poorly-conceived strike should fail. It will fail if you continue to stand united." But the Newark Teachers Association, NEA's affiliate, chose to "unite" by going out on strike two months later—in February, 1966— and for virtually the same reasons the union did.

Despite its public statement, NEA was moving toward a position favoring some strikes. In his speech to the 1966 NEA convention, Carr spoke again on this matter: "Strikes and threats of strikes should not be a requirement for successful agreement between responsible boards of education and responsible education associations. There is an urgent need to explore complex ethical, political, economic, and legal problems relating to the work stoppage. . . . Under what conditions, if any, could a strike be considered necessary? Under what conditions is a strike specifically unprofessional and unethical? Should professional discipline be applied in the event of an improper work stoppage?"

AND MORE STRIKES

The number of teacher strikes increased again in 1967—from 33 to 105. Although these strikes were not limited to large cities, it was the urban teacher who led the way. Members of the Federation of Teachers in Detroit, for example, struck for two weeks in September. They voted 5,036 to 113 to reject a contract offered by the board of education and to seek a larger salary increase. The union asked for a $1,700 across the board increase; the board offered $500. The board raised its offer to $600; the union lowered its demands to $1,200. Then the teachers went on strike. After the schools were closed for two weeks, the teachers and the board agreed to a compromise package giving teachers $1,700 increases, but during a two-year period.

So in 1967 the dam broke. Teachers' strikes, now numbering more than 100 a year, gave the associations and the unions little choice but to endorse this militancy. Until 1967 strikes were not officially acceptable to the NEA under any conditions, though this had not prevented the association from supporting affiliates who had struck. On July 1, 1967, the NEA Board of Directors received a report from a committee it had appointed to study impasses in negotiation situations. The committee presented both a majority and a minority report. The minority position—favoring strikes—was argued persuasively by Fred Hipp, executive secretary of the New Jersey Education Association, and by Janet Dean, president of the Dade County (Florida) Classroom Teachers Association. After long debate the board voted down a motion that would have put the association on record as not recommending the strike. Then it approved the minority position—supporting affiliates who strike. The resolution listed procedures to be used in ending an impasse between teachers associations and their employers: mediation, fact-finding, arbitration, political action, and sanctions. The resolution then reflected a new stand on strikes. "The NEA believes that the above procedures should make the strike unnecessary. The NEA recommends that every effort be made to avoid the strike as a procedure for the resolution of impasse. The NEA recognizes that under conditions of severe stress, causing deterioration of the educational program, and when good faith attempts at resolution have been rejected, strikes have occurred and may occur in the future. In such instances, the NEA will offer all of the services at its command to the affiliate concerned to help resolve the impasse." During the 1967 NEA convention, executive secretary-elect Sam M. Lambert summarized the action, saying, "The NEA will not encourage strikes, but if one occurs after all good faith efforts fail, we will not walk out on our local associations."

Several state affiliates of the NEA had taken similar positions. The Massachusetts Teachers Association, at its May, 1967, convention, voted approval of the right of teachers to strike. The New Jersey Education Association's executive secretary was a leading spokesman for the changed NEA position. The Maryland State Teachers Association (MSTA) in October following the NEA convention approved a policy similar to the NEA statement, saying: "MSTA strongly recommends that every effort be made to avoid the withholding of professional services as a procedure for the resolution of impasse; however, if such an event takes place, MSTA, in accepting its obligations to support its members and its affiliates, will use all the resources at its command to help resolve the situation." Only one state group, the Wyoming affiliate, went on record as opposing the new policy.

Although the total number of teacher strikes in 1968 was fewer than in 1967, the vast numbers involved ran the total of idle teaching days to an all-time high of 2,190,000—more than twice the working days lost in any previous year in the nation's history. And the 1968 strikes were varied. Some, as in Florida and New York City, involved thousands of educators, while others were quite small. One strike actually involved one teacher. This mini-strike took place on Matinicus Island, Maine, in March. The only teacher in the island's only school gave his 16 pupils a week's homework in advance, then walked out to protest what he called "deplorable conditions." The school district immediately fired him and hired another teacher. The strike, the fired teacher said, "did serve to further the cause of the children's education. Townspeople already agreed informally to build a new $30,000 school. The action will be formalized at the annual town meeting later this month." The strike, he said, "put some grease in the gears."

But most strikes during 1968 put large numbers of teachers on the bricks. In Montgomery County, Maryland, an affluent suburb of Washington, D.C., 5,000 teachers affiliated with NEA struck for six days to win higher pay. NEA officials from the nearby headquarters urged the strike, with NEA's president telling the teachers, "Nothing less than closing the schools will work." After six days of the strike, the county school board approved an additional $2.7 million for salaries, agreed to a "no reprisals" clause, and accepted payroll deduction for Montgomery County Education Association dues. The strike received nationwide attention when NBC-TV commentator David Brinkley dramatized its salary increase issue on a television news show. Said Brinkley: "By some measurements Montgomery County, Maryland, a suburb of Washington, is the richest county in the United States. Its taxes are high, and the schools are considered good. Today its schools have closed because the teachers are on strike. Among other things they want more money—a starting salary of $6,600 a year. In New York City, the garbagemen are on strike demanding $7,024 a year. They've been offered $6,800. The teachers in the richest county in the United States are on strike trying to get $200 a year less than New York City had offered its garbagemen. Good night, Chet."

Other 1968 strikes: Washington, D.C., schools were closed March 7 by the union so teachers could assemble and march to Congress to demand higher pay (District of Columbia teachers' salaries are set by Congress). In Pennsylvania, 18 strikes were led by teacher groups between April 28 and June 9. Salaries were the predominant issue. In Pittsburgh, the Federation of Teachers led a 10-day strike in March. The union's demand for a bargaining election was answered by a promise that such an election was likely under pending state legislation. In Woodbridge, New Jersey, a union-led strike resulted in the jailing of one of the American Federation of Teachers' field representatives and the local union president. The AFT field man served 60 days, the president 25. "Jail only strengthens us," they said on the front page of the AFT journal. Later in the year the Woodbridge Federation of Teachers won a representation election, defeating the Woodbridge Education Association, an NEA affiliate. The union credited the publicity about the jailings for rallying teachers to its side.

The public, now aware of teacher strikes because of their numbers and publicity, said it opposed them. A Gallup Poll published in March, 1968, showed that 57 percent of those interviewed said public school teachers should not be permitted to strike. A similar poll taken in December showed a slight increase, with 60 percent saying teachers should not be permitted to strike. The percentage of teachers approving strikes by teachers was 68.2, according to the NEA research division. In 1965, 53.3 percent of teachers had favored strikes. Perhaps because of its increasing approval by teachers, NEA's Representative Assembly, meeting in July, 1968, approved a resolution on "withdrawal of services." The resolution reiterated the position taken by the NEA Board of Directors the preceding year which had suggested mediation, fact-finding, voluntary arbitration, political action, and sanctions for ending an impasse between teachers and employers. Then the 1967 resolution had added, "Under conditions of severe stress causing deterioration of the educational program, and when good faith attempts at resolution have been rejected, strikes have occurred and may occur in the future." In these cases, the 1967 resolution stated, "The Association will offer all of the services at its command to the affiliate concerned to help resolve the impasse." At the July, 1968, meeting the NEA assembly also added another sentence aimed at the use of strikebreakers: "The Association denounces the practice of staffing schools with any personnel when, in an effort to provide high quality education, educators withdraw their services."

The number of teacher strikes set another record during the 1968-69 school year. From August, 1968 through June, 1969, an all-time high of 131 strikes was recorded by NEA's research division. These strikes took place in 24 states and in the District of Columbia. The number of days of work time lost during that school year was 2.7 million, the research division said, but added that the figure was less than 1 percent of the total time devoted to public school teaching during the year. During the 1969–70 school year, the number of strikes rose even higher—to 171. This pattern of teacher strikes at a relatively high level, but never more than 1 percent of all teacher time, continued into the 1970s. The strikers' demands still centered on three issues: higher pay, a greater say in school planning and curriculum development, and the right to organize.

Some strikes were aggravated when unions and associations, competing for teacher votes in the same school district, tried to outdo one another in militancy. The common tactic was to accuse the majority group, usually the association, of inaction and lack of guts. This pushed the challenged group into greater militancy. In such a battle, the smaller groups had little to lose. If the greater militancy resulted in higher pay or greater benefits for teachers, the minority group claimed it was the force behind the new militancy; should the militancy fail, the minority group then called for teachers to rally around it, to leave the ineffective majority. Exactly how many unnecessary strikes were forced by this tactic is unknown, but it is likely that sophisticated negotiation, in an atmosphere free of competition between organizing unions, would have resulted in fewer strikes and a smoother path for some teachers and school boards. Los Angeles provides an example. In 1969 the Los Angeles Association of Classroom Teachers, an affiliate of NEA and of the California Teachers Association, had recruited 19,200 members in the city. The Los Angeles Federation of Teachers had enrolled only 3,000 members. When it became known that an additional $3 million for special education programs was available to the school board, the Association of Classroom Teachers, competing with the growing union, threatened to strike for higher pay. The union backed the strike, which lasted only one day. Nothing resulted from the work stoppage; the special education money was not made available to teachers for salaries; but the association and the union had begun public sparring. In May, 1970, Los Angeles teachers again went on strike. This time the association and the union agreed to merge into a new group, United Teachers of Los Angeles. The second strike was much longer—five weeks. But this strike was also unsuccessful. After claims and counterclaims stretching for five weeks, the school board offered about $13 million for teacher salaries, announcing that the funds would come from money earmarked for educational improvements. The teachers could not decide whether to accept the offer and seem money-grubbing or to stay on strike for more money from different funds. In the end, they did neither; by a vote of 4,964 to 3,714 they decided to go back to their classrooms and refuse the board's offer. They got nothing, but claimed they had led a "moral crusade" to show the citizens of the city how great were the educational needs of the schools. In both strikes, competing organizational priorities and personalities had meant more than gains for teachers. And, though teacher unity was the motto of both groups, no unity had been achieved. In contrast stands the Denver strike during the same school year. Denver teachers, members of the NEA and its state affiliate, struck November 17, 1969. On November 31 they voted to accept a school board offer of salary gains that allowed Denver teachers to earn as much as $15,000 a year. The key was unity: the Denver teachers were able to strike for a clear goal without any association-union rivalry, and they made clear gains.

STRIKES LEGALIZED

During the late 1960s strikes by teachers were illegal in every state. The courts, following precedents set in strikes involving firemen, policemen, and other municipal workers, in general had ruled that teachers could not strike, could not disrupt the public order. Although strikes took place anyway, teachers and teacher groups often were hauled into court and slapped with injunctions and fines. Teacher-leaders thought that the courts were on the "establishment" side and against the teacher-worker. In 1970 this began to change. Early that year the NEA affiliate in Hawaii announced that it had lobbied successfully, with NEA help, to gain passage of a state law allowing teachers and public employees the same right to strike as private employees. The law provided for arbitration and mediation, but should that fail, the law allowed the ultimate weapon. Hawaiian and NEA officials predicted that such laws would mean fewer strikes, not more. NEA's general counsel hailed the Hawaii law as "a major breakthrough in the field of public employee bargaining" and said that in certain respects the law was the "most progressive public employee law ever enacted in the nation." In October another state, Pennsylvania, passed a similar law. Now two states officially allowed teacher strikes, and one more, Vermont, had legislation limiting the use of injunctions against teachers in a strike. NEA continued through the early 1970s to press for more such laws, including a federal bargaining law for public employees. In 1970 the NEA Representative Assembly voted to urge its members and affiliates to seek "state legislation that clearly and firmly mandates the adoption of professional negotiation agreements."

Ironically, Hawaiian teachers had to call a strike to win

112

their first contract under the 1970 law. After nearly two years of reorganizing and negotiating, the Hawaii State Teachers Association called a statewide strike (again with heavy NEA assistance). Minutes before a midnight deadline on February 17, 1972, the association got a firm offer in writing from the state board. In retrospect, it was obvious that what caused the Hawaii strike was the very fact that the state had an advanced, progressive law. The hitch was that few believed it except the teachers themselves. It took patience and a near-strike to convince the state establishment that the law really meant what it said: that teacher groups and board officials must sit down and work out a written contract on salaries, class size, fringe benefits, and other matters. It is doubly ironic that it was in Pennsylvania—where the second state law was passed to allow teacher strikes—that the most disastrous strike of the early 1970s occurred. Teachers in Philadelphia had voted to oust the old Philadelphia Teachers Association and to be represented by an American Federation of Teachers local. The union got no bargain when it won the right to negotiate for Philadelphia's teachers, however, for the city was going broke and no amount of militancy would be able to change that. The strike began on Labor Day, 1972—schools never opened for classes that fall— and lasted more than 10 weeks. The strike was legal, thanks to the new law. But while the law upheld the right to strike, it did not mandate money for the schools. Philadelphia had gone into the 1972–73 school year with a $52 million budget deficit. To help save money, the school board wanted to cut the teaching force by 485. The union, in addition to declaring the staff cut impossible, demanded a 34 percent pay raise. The impasse was real. The city could not even borrow money; because of its known deficit, its rating by Standard and Poor's was so low no one would lend it money. It was a classic conflict in what had become a classic problem of urban areas in the 1970s. Cities, having lost revenue through fleeing population and facing massive problems of high social costs, turned to the state governments for financial aid. (In Philadelphia, the city fathers asked Harrisburg for $40 million; they got $12 million.) Then both state and city turned to the federal government for more. But federal aid to education throughout the early 1970s remained at about 7 percent of all school costs. The cupboard was bare. In Philadelphia, the strike was an all-around disaster: members lost 10 week's pay, students lost 10 week's education, and the city had its poverty exposed to the nation. The teachers returned to their schools empty-handed and bitter, and the city's lack of funds persisted. By 1974 Philadelphia was projecting a $32 million school budget deficit.

This pattern reoccurred in 1974 in Baltimore. Teachers there had voted in 1973 to return the Public School Teachers Association (PSTA) to negotiation power. PSTA had lost the city's teachers to an AFT union for six years, but urban problems being what they were, the union was unable to deliver substantial improvements for teachers and they voted PSTA back in. PSTA called a strike in the spring of 1974. It lasted about a month, and when teachers went back they had won a promise of a 3 percent raise, to be followed by a 6 percent raise in the coming school year. Although PSTA, with help from NEA and the Maryland State Teachers Association, had done a commendable job representing the teachers (especially in contrast to the bitter and divisive Philadelphia strike), the city was still unable to do much for the teachers. As in Philadelphia, the city turned to the state government for help. Annapolis promised some funds, but they were not nearly enough to meet the 11 percent raise demand of the teachers. So a weak settlement, which spokesmen for the teachers called "palatable," resulted, and teachers got increases less than inflation growth, then estimated at 8.8 percent a year.

Teachers in major cities faced this critical question every time they negotiated or struck: Where was the money going to come from? A 1974 publication of the National Urban Coalition, *Urban Schools and School Finance Reform: Promise and Reality*, by Callahan, Wilkin, and Sillerman, pointed out that the nation's 44 largest cities had extraordinary demands for

114

noneducational services as compared to suburban and rural areas. Per capita police expenditures were 53 percent higher than corresponding state averages; fire protection services were 91 percent higher; refuse disposal expenditures were 87 percent greater. These higher costs, in turn, led to lower funding of city education. "While central cities in the nation's 36 largest metropolitan areas allocate 33 percent of their budget for education, many of their suburban neighbors devote 55 to 60 percent of their local budgets to educational programs," according to John J. Callahan, principal author of the coalition publication. Callahan noted that excessively high tax rates led to a treadmill of events which cancelled out the raising of taxes for education or any other pressing need. "By further raising taxes, cities are promoting the continued flight of middle- and upper-income families and taxable property values from city areas," he said. "That loss of tax base, in turn, creates further fiscal pressure on the remaining city tax base." In light of this familiar chain of events, the coalition publication suggested that city teachers change their focus from dwindling city coffers to state and federal legislation designed to abandon the regressive property tax financing system through fiscal reform. The coalition authors suggested that school finance reformers: 1) Be aware of the cumulative and interrelated need, cost, wealth, and tax effort differentials that cities face when financing their school systems; 2) incorporate factors which reflect the real costs of education such as the higher price a district must pay for a common educational service and requirements for supportive educational inputs that are present in the district, but not necessarily in other school districts throughout the state; 3) seek finances from state and local revenue sources that do not aggravate the fiscal burdens of low-income populations, particularly those residing in large cities; 4) design aid systems that account for total urban tax burdens; and 5) keep in mind that with expanded state aid, development of an open-ended percentage equalization policy, and the use of a composite fiscal "deservedness" index, a state would be in a position to channel its external aid to those districts that are most in need of such resources. Until reforms as extensive as these are undertaken, however, teachers in Philadelphia, Baltimore, and other large cities will continue to beat their heads against a wall every time they make demands for higher salaries and costly school improvements. Given the low percentage of federal aid to schools, the prognosis is not good.

Organized Teacher militancy has a long and varied history.
Above, Chicago teachers demonstrate in the early 1930s. (NEA)

In the early days of the nation, each community maintained a continuous interest in the behavior of its teachers both in and out of school. Here, community leaders quiz students to evaluate their teachers. (NEA)

National Teachers Association President John Philbrick was typical of early leaders in that he believed teachers could not improve their lot until the schools themselves improved. "The proper means should be employed to secure continued self-improvement of teachers; and with this view they should, as far as practicable, be commended, promoted, and regarded in proportion to their advancement. . . ." (NEA)

William McAndrew

James Cruikshank

During the first years of teacher organizations, these two men had this dialogue: MC ANDREW: "And how long before you advanced from high-hat meetings to the practical improvement of teachers?" CRUIKSHANK: "Gradually. There was, at the start, too much *why*, not enough *what*, and hardly any *how* at all. Even the most practical schoolmen, when asked to prepare addresses, suffered an attack of pedantry and soared to cloudland." (NEA)

United States Commissioner of Education William T. Harris told teachers in 1905 that "the teacher whose salary is low . . . will try to improve his skill in teaching. . . . What teacher could not improve his position and find a more adequate salary for himself?" (NEA)

Ella Flagg Young, later the first woman president of the National Education Association, told teachers in 1907 that they must grasp a greater role in their profession. "Can it be true that teachers are stronger in their work when they have no voice in the planning of the great issues committed to their hands?" she asked. (NEA)

J. W. Crabtree, hired as secretary of the National Education Association in 1917, set as his first task a membership campaign to make NEA representative of classroom teachers. In his years of stewardship, the association grew many times over. (NEA)

Donald DuShane, National Education Association president in 1941, helped create the association's National Commission for the Defense of Democracy through Education. In 1943, the commission set up a fund to defend teachers, a fund later named the DuShane Emergency Fund for Teacher Rights. (NEA)

In the 1960s, National Education Association salary schools evolved into negotiation training sessions. When NEA's annual salary school was held in 1964, more than 200 delegates representing 47 states came to Washington, D.C., to learn negotiation skills. (NEA)

Ester Wilfong   George Jones

As schools were desegregated in the 1950s and 1960s, teacher
associations in the South merged, and black leaders were asked
to serve national roles. Ester Wilfong of the state of Washington
served on the NEA Executive Committee in the 1960s; George
Jones became an NEA staff director. By 1974, NEA had elected
both a black woman and a black man as president. (NEA)

In the early 1970s, the National Education Association joined
with the American Federation of State, County, and Municipal
Employees (AFL–CIO) to form the Coalition of American Public
Employees. *Above,* AFSCME President Jerry Wurf *(center)* and
NEA President Helen Bain announce the new coalition. (NEA)

By 1973, the National Education Association had begun political action programs—local and state groups of teachers that
worked for election of pro-education candidates. *Above,* NEA
President Catharine Barrett talks with Senator Walter Mondale
and NEA aides. In 1976, NEA teachers had a mechanism for
endorsement of a Presidential candidate. (NEA)

Albert Shanker, now president of the American Federation of Teachers, saw his star begin to rise after New York City teachers chose his local union as their representative in 1961. Later he directed a merger of AFT and NEA teachers in New York State and emerged as one of the most powerful teacher-leaders in the nation. (AFT)

An estimated 35,000 Florida teachers jammed the Tangerine
Bowl in Orlando in 1967 to protest poor financing of state
schools. The Florida Education Association invoked "sanctions" against the state that year. (NEA)

By the mid-1970s teachers had begun joint action with other organized groups of American labor. Joint strike actions occurred, and more commonly *(as above),* teachers marched in support of colleagues in other unions. Teachers seemed to have learned that they must face the future side by side with other blocs of Americans. (NEA)

10 / Teacher Negotiations:

Power Formalized

THROUGHOUT THE 1960s and into the 1970s, teachers went on strike for many reasons and with increasing frequency. These strikes, often the only sign of militancy noticed by the public and the press, hid a more important aspect of teacher militancy: the development of mechanisms to win written contracts for teachers. Thousands of teachers were involved in strikes in these years; hundreds of thousands were being covered by contracts that gave them, often for the first time, clear-cut rights and benefits.

NEA's salary schools evolved into negotiation training sessions during this period. At NEA's annual salary school in 1964, more than 200 delegates representing 47 states came to Washington to discover that their four days were to be spent learning negotiation skills, not salary scheduling. To back up its efforts to encourage negotiation by its local affiliates, NEA had by February, 1964, distributed 73,000 copies of its *Guidelines for Professional Negotiations*. By November, 1964, NEA reported that an estimated 100,000 teachers in 346 districts were serving under written negotiation agreements. States leading in the number of such agreements were California (with 159), Connecticut (70), Washington (26), Oregon (20), and New Jersey (17). NEA negotiation specialists categorized these agreements into three types—levels I, II, III. A level I agreement merely provided for recognition of the local association or union as the negotiation agent. A level II agreement included recognition and also established a definite procedure for resolution of impasse between the school board and the teacher group. A level III agreement went further, guaranteeing arbitration or conciliation to resolve impasses and spelling out detailed policies. Of the 346 agreements recorded in November, 1964, 101 were level I, 87 were level II, and 158 were level III.

By May, 1967, NEA reported that nearly 400,000 school personnel were represented by its affiliates under agreements in 1,179 school systems. Further, NEA reported, AFT-affiliated teachers were working under contracts in 35 additional school systems. In October, 1967, the NEA Research Division published an analysis of 1,540 negotiation agreements on file in its office. Not all of these agreements were ideal, either from the teacher point of view or from the viewpoint of the school board. The NEA Research Division noted, for example, that some agreements were merely "recognition" agreements—level I. But other agreements did spell out procedures for negotiation (level II), and still others included a mechanism for resolution of impasse and even covered substantive matters such as salary schedules, leave policies, and other negotiated items (level III).

NEGOTIATION LAWS

This continuing growth in negotiated agreements was in large part due to the increase in statewide teacher negotiation laws. Laws mandating school board-teacher organization negotiation were in effect by 1965 in Connecticut and Washington and, in addition, in Michigan teacher representation elections were held under labor laws. Before 1965 three states had passed negotiation laws—Alaska in 1959, New Hampshire in 1955, and Wisconsin in 1962. By the end of 1965, teacher negotiation laws had also passed in California, Florida, Massachusetts, New Jersey, and Oregon. New Jersey and Massachusetts laws went into effect in 1966. The laws varied considerably. Florida's was a simple section of the state school code permitting school boards to recognize teachers committees. The entire relevant section reads:

Section 230.23. Powers and Duties of County Board. The county board, after considering recommendations submitted by the county superintendent, shall exercise the following general powers: 1. Determine Policies. The county board shall determine and adopt such policies as are deemed necessary by it for the efficient operation and general improvement of the county school system. In arriving at a determination of policies affecting certificated personnel, the county board may appoint or recognize existing committees composed of members of the teaching profession, as defined in the professional teaching practices act, sections 231.54–59, Florida Statutes. When such committees are involved in the consideration of policies for resolving problems or reaching agreements affecting certificated personnel, the committee membership shall include certificated personnel representing all work levels of such instructional and administrative personnel as defined in the school code.

A new collective bargaining law replaced this Florida act in 1975.

More typical of the state negotiation laws was the Connecticut act, which placed the right to be recognized upon the teachers' group, not leaving it to the whim of the school board. The Connecticut bill, which became law in June, 1965, provided for classroom teachers and administrators to negotiate through one all-inclusive group or through two separate representation units, whichever the majority decided by secret ballot. It made provision for the execution of written group contracts incorporating agreements reached by teachers with boards of education. The bill specifically prohibited strikes, in line with Connecticut Education Association policy at the time, but offered the alternative of mediation by the state commissioner of education. If this failed, the bill further provided for referral of disagreements to a three-member advisory board of arbitrators; one member would be named by each party and the third would be selected by the first two.

In Wisconsin, Michigan, and Massachusetts, the negotiation laws affecting teachers were labor laws, designed to deal with municipal employees. Under these laws, groups of teachers were defined as falling within the meaning of "labor organization." Wisconsin's law, for example, included these sections:

2. Rights of municipal employees. Municipal employees shall have the right of self-organization, to affiliate with labor organizations of their own choosing and the right to be represented by labor organizations of their own choice in conferences and negotiations with their municipal employers or their representatives on questions of wages, hours, and conditions of employment, and such employees shall have the rights to refrain from any and all such activities. . . . (d) Collective bargaining units. Whenever a question arises between a municipal employer and a labor union as to whether the union represents the employees or the employer, either the union or the municipality may petition the Wisconsin Labor Relations Board to conduct an election among said employees to determine whether they desire to be represented by a labor organization. . . . (i) Agreements. Upon the completion of negotiations with a labor organization representing a majority of the employees in a collective bargaining unit, if a settlement is reached, the employer shall reduce the same to writing either in the form of an ordinance, resolution or agreement. Such agreement may include a term for which it shall remain in effect not to exceed one year. . . .

The Wisconsin law also provided for fact-finding and mediation in the event of impasse between employee group and employer.

Another type of statewide negotiation law was typified by

the California Winton Act, which removed teachers from the public employees act and placed them under a new law specifically designed for teachers and school districts. It added educational matters as subjects for negotiation as well as matters of salaries and working conditions, and uniquely, provided for school board negotiation through a new unit: a negotiating council made up of representatives of teacher groups in proportion to their membership. Varying patterns of participation and membership occurred as the Winton Act went into effect. In most districts, teachers groups so small that qualification for council membership was doubtful did not apply for representation. In Los Angeles, however, 16 groups applied for seats on the two councils (one for the city unified district, the other for the junior college district). On the Los Angeles Unified District Negotiation Council, four seats each went to the Los Angeles Teachers Association and the Affiliated Teacher Organizations of Los Angeles, and the ninth seat went to the AFT Local 1021. California teachers found the Winton Act unmanageable in the long run, however, and in the mid-1970s lobbied for full bargaining rights under a new state law that would set up a single bargaining agent in each school district. It passed in 1976.

Bills to bring guaranteed negotiation rights to teachers were considered by legislators in Illinois, Indiana, Minnesota, New Mexico, Ohio, and Rhode Island during 1965. By March, 1967, eight states (California, Connecticut, Massachusetts, Michigan, Oregon, Rhode Island, Washington, and Wisconsin) had laws mandating that some type of teacher-school board negotiation take place. Three additional states (Alaska, Florida, and New Hampshire) had laws permitting such negotiations. Further, 11 states had legislation under consideration: Delaware, Illinois, Indiana, Kentucky, Maine, Maryland, Nebraska, New York, Ohio, Oklahoma, and Texas. A Nebraska law passed by a slim margin and went into effect in September, 1967. Supported by the Nebraska State Education Association and the Nebraska State School Boards Association, the law was permissive but incorporated required-action provisions to such an extent that the state association considered it mandatory for all practical purposes. Under the law, the teacher group that enrolled a majority of the certificated staff for the preceding two years had to be recognized by the school board. Good-faith negotiations were called for, and all negotiating school boards were required to reach mutually acceptable agreement and to produce written agreements signed by both parties. The law also incorporated a procedure for fact-finding in cases of impasse. Early in 1967, the Minnesota State Supreme Court ruled that exclusion of teachers from the state's public employee negotiating law was constitutional. The Minnesota Education Association then drafted legislation which called for the mandating of separate teacher-school board negotiation. The Minnesota legislature passed a compromise bill, but one that did mandate bargaining between school boards and teachers. It limited the matters that could be negotiated mainly to economic matters and required that, if competing teacher groups existed, a five-member teachers council, with proportionate representation from each group, must be established.

Although NEA affiliates and teacher unions often argued about the nature of state legislation requiring teacher bargaining, both worked for some such laws. The AFL-CIO, eager to recruit white-collar workers, also was lobbying for legislation mandating negotiations for all public employees. At the 1967 convention of the AFL-CIO, the union passed a resolution reasserting its support of the right of state and local government employees to organize into unions of their choice for the purpose of collective bargaining. "We reassert our belief that the realistic vehicle for state and local government labor relations is collective bargaining, together with effective mediation and fact-finding procedures," it said, "including the use of impartial fact-finding panels with authority to make recommendations for settlement."

A sidelight on school negotiations—agency shop—developed mainly in Michigan. In 1967 teachers there negotiated several agreements which included this aspect of labor law. In teacher agreements such clauses are generally labeled "financial responsibility," and they require any teacher not joining the organization that is recognized as the exclusive bargaining agent to "execute an authorization for the deduction of a sum equivalent to the dues and assessments of the association which sum shall be forwarded to the dues and assessments of the association to cover the expenses of negotiation processes." In Warren, Michigan, an unaffiliated teacher challenged the legality of the agency shop clause, but the challenge was dismissed by the Michigan Circuit Court for the County of Macomb in July, 1968.

When the 1968–69 school year began, 43 percent (2,624) of the school systems in the United States enrolling 1,000 or more pupils had negotiation procedures or agreements. In these districts, affiliates of NEA were the negotiators in 92 percent or 2,337 school systems. Slightly more than one million instructional staff members were employed in the systems with agreements. NEA affiliates negotiated for 745,262 of these staff members, AFT for 181,388.

During 1968, legislation authorizing teacher-school board negotiations had become law in two more states—Maryland and New Jersey. Maryland's negotiation statute, signed into law in May, provided for exclusive representation by one teacher group, with the representative chosen by election if necessary; no more than two representation units in any school system; prohibition of strikes; and establishment of an impasse resolution panel. New Jersey's statute, which became law after both houses of the state legislature overruled the governor's veto in September, 1968, provided public employees with a separate administrative agency, a Public Employment Relations Commission. The commission was empowered to make policy, establish rules and regulations, mediate impasses, and resolve representation disputes. The bill provided for exclusive representation by an appropriate unit which could be selected, designated, or elected by the majority of employees. Steps toward negotiation statutes were taken in six additional states in 1968. In North Dakota, South Dakota, and Vermont, bills were being drafted. In Pennsylvania, both the state education association and the Pennsylvania Federation of Teachers were sponsoring legislation, the former calling for a professional negotiation bill and the latter a public employee collective bargaining bill. In Ohio, the state education association had appeared before a legislative committee studying professional negotiation; further hearings were planned to draw up guidelines for legislation. And in Hawaii, the state education association presented to the legislature and the governor a proposal to change the state constitution to permit collective bargaining by public employees. In Iowa, a district court ruled in 1968 that "in the absence of statute, public employees do have the power to engage in collective bargaining and to enter into collective bargaining agreements." In Kentucky, the legislature defeated a teacher-school board bargaining bill. The bill passed the state house, but died in the state senate.

Two judicial decisions affecting teacher-school board negotiations were made in Michigan during 1968. The state's Labor Mediation Board ruled, in the fall of 1968, that there was no conflict between the state's teacher tenure act and the agency shop requirements in some 100 contracts negotiated in the state. The board rejected a school board's argument that the agency shop requirement, demanding that a teacher join the bargaining organization or pay a fee to it equal to the dues, would be contrary to the tenure law prohibition on deducting dues without authorization. This was not relevant because, the board said, "The association had not requested such deduction without authorization. Rather, it had proposed that teachers be required either to sign a dues deduction authorization or pay 'the sum equivalent through some other means.'" The other Michigan decision was made by the state supreme court, which ruled, in a case involving teachers in Holland, Michigan, that issuing an injunction to force teachers to stop striking was justified only if boards of education had exhausted all avenues

of good faith negotiations or if evidence of "violence, irrepara-
ble injury, or breach of the peace" was presented to lower
courts. The decision in effect stated that school boards could
not immediately and freely win an injunction to stop a strike.
NEA had filed an *amicus curiae* brief in the case. The
Michigan Education Association's Office of Professional Negotiations said, "The general effect of this historic ruling is a
sweeping reversal of previously held opinions that injunctions
would be issued automatically if public employees were engaged in concerted activity to withhold services. . . . The
decision established a bill of rights not only of teachers, but for
all public employees in the State of Michigan." Thus by 1969
the trend to authorized negotiation by teachers and other
public employees was irreversible. Cornell Law School negotiation expert Walter E. Oberer told an NEA seminar in August,
1969, "There will be more of it (negotiation), more statutes
authorizing it, more employees engaged in it."

THE ADMINISTRATOR'S ROLE

One additional aspect of negotiation received considerable attention in the late 1960s: the role of the school
administrator. The three major national school administrator
groups (the American Association of School Administrators, the
National Association of Secondary School Principals, and the
National Association of Elementary School Principals) included the topic in their convention programs in 1968. In
addition, AASA published a book, *The School Administrator
and Negotiation.* The forward to that book places the situation
facing administrators in focus:

This new form of staff-administration-board interaction has become firmly rooted as a "way of life" in the public school
enterprise. This is not to say, however, that these accords have been
achieved without some tension, misunderstanding—even rancor—
or without the expenditure of long hours of diligent dialogue and
exhausting effort. . . . The complexity, newness, and ultimate

135

uncertainties of the negotiation process—frustrating as they are now or may become—are not likely to deter the onward press of teachers to share in planning for decision making on a widening range of educational matters. The times point in this direction . . . the trend toward its spread is unmistakable.

The AASA volume then went on to give school administrators' suggestions for carrying out negotiations.

Despite the pain evidenced by school superintendents over the negotiation process, their role at least was fairly clear. In most cases, they were "management"; indeed, negotiation laws usually excluded them from the bargaining unit. But what of the middle administrators—the principals? Their role was not at all fixed or certain, and they received conflicting advice. NEA President Braulio Alonso, himself a principal, urged those attending the 1968 convention of the National Association of Secondary School Principals to join with teachers: "In many places the principals stood with teachers," he said. "In others, the principal sided with the school board. In every case where the principals did not support the teachers, the principals have been the losers." Other authorities urged principals to demand separate treatment. A New Jersey school administrator urged them to "get in on the ground floor of legislation in negotiation. Principals should make certain that state legislation gives them the right to bargain separately." Still another piece of advice came from a Michigan superintendent of schools, who argued that the principal was a key member of the administrative staff and must be given the responsibility and authority to carry out his function as a member of management. The principal or administrator, as a member of the management team, is represented directly on the negotiation team, he continued, and has the opportunity to refine administrative proposals and to counter teacher proposals that are not in the best interest of the school system. But George Redfern, associate secretary of AASA, thought the principal's role was not so clear. "Principals are uncertain about their roles in negotiation," he said. "Are they bystanders or participators? . . . Principals may develop many doubts about the ultimate shape and form of their position." Further, he said, "Many principals are concerned not only about their roles in negotiation but also about how they are to be represented in the negotiating unit. Some are included in the teacher unit; others are excluded deliberately."

One group of principals decided, in 1968, that they would bargain for themselves. The Michigan Elementary School Principals Association disaffiliated itself from the Michigan Education Association after the state labor relations board ruled that principals could not be represented by teacher groups at the bargaining table. A similar situation occurred in Minnesota the same year, though the principals' organization did not leave the state education association. Instead, the principals were able to encourage the Minnesota Education Association to devote more effort toward negotiating for them. Some administrators resolved the question of their role in negotiations by joining a union that would compete with the American Federation of Teachers. About 200 principals in New York City joined Teamsters Local 237 in 1968, claiming that they were concerned about the weakening of the merit system and about the loss of their authority. The Philadelphia Principals Association, 300 strong, announced in July, 1968, that it too was considering organizing a local within the Teamsters Union. Teamsters Union acting president Frank E. Fitzsimmons said in June, 1968, that his union was actively seeking to organize public employees. "We are organizing them, accepting them as members, and representing them vigorously," he said. By the fall of 1971 there were locals of the School Administrators and Supervisors Organizing Committee, AFL-CIO, in New York City, Chicago, Boston, Providence, San Francisco, and Washington, D.C. The group was chartered by AFL-CIO president George Meany in April, 1971.

BARGAINING LAW

Another action enhanced the teachers' right to bargain in the late 1960s. In June, 1968, the United States Court of Appeals for the Seventh Circuit ruled that the Constitution gave teachers the right to engage in union activities. Further, the court said that a teacher might not be dismissed for exercising this right, whether or not he had tenure. As the 1960s came to an end, however, the teachers' right to strike remained limited through the absence of laws in most states and through state laws denying this right to all public employees in a few states. The Taylor Law in New York State, passed in 1967, was an example of the latter. It has been condemned and praised, for it has brought to attention the crucial issue in all such laws: Where do the constitutional rights of the teacher clash with the rights of the public? The author of the legislation, George W. Taylor, argued that the essence of a good law in this area (and he believed the Taylor Law was a good law) was that it brought people together under enforced negotiation. "This is a matter of human relations, not legalistic solutions," he said. It is a difficult and complex matter, he said, because the choice is not between good and evil but between good and good—between the rights of the teachers and the rights of the public. Veteran labor reporter A. H. Raskin agreed with Taylor that the law was the "best bet" for resolving labor disputes in public employment. The Taylor Law, he said, "offers the fullest opportunity for bringing into the civil-service the practices that are normal in labor-management relations generally, while insuring that the workers will get a neutral verdict on their demands if they are not satisfied with what comes out of direct negotiations." He concluded, "No law will produce absolute insurance. That is unattainable even in a police state. But the community cannot tolerate the notion that it is helpless at the hands of organized workers to whom it has entrusted responsibility for essential functions. If the rule of law cannot be made to work in this field, what hope is there for preserving it against the assaults of the rootless and the disaffected in the slums and all the other areas on the outskirts of hope?" On the other hand, some labor law experts and some representatives of teacher groups have found the Taylor Law less than ideal. Theodore W. Kheel, an experienced mediator in the public-service arena, said in 1968 that the Taylor Law, by totally forbidding strikes, invited unions to threaten to strike. The fault, he said, is "that the law appears to invite unions to threaten to violate the law, by prohibiting strikes of public employees, [and] the law eliminates collective bargaining which implies the right of the buyer or seller to refuse to buy or sell by a strike or a lockout. You can't bargain unless you have the right to say 'no deal' and not buy the car." A spokesman for the organized teachers' point of view, New York attorney Donald H. Wollett, attacked the Taylor Law because, though it called for fact-finding, it did not require that the fact-finder's recommendations be followed. "Unless the strike prohibition of the law is ignored," he said, "the employee organization cannot, as a practical matter, reject the recommendations of the fact-finder." Wollett concluded that there were two alternatives to correct this weakness in the Taylor Law: provide for compulsory arbitration or legalize public employee strikes. He said he preferred the latter. Whether laws like the Taylor Law can, in the long run, provide effective solutions to teacher-school board conflicts is uncertain. Clearly such laws have failed to prevent teacher strikes. New York teachers struck several times before and after the Taylor Law was passed. Similar laws in other states have failed to prevent teacher walkouts. Further, in the 1970s federal employees unions and the National Education Association were seeking a national law that would require public employers to negotiate with their employees. Such a law could override state statutes, provide for compulsory arbitration, and/or authorize strikes under some conditions.

State laws continued to change in the 1970s and the changes favored the teacher's right to bargain. In addition to the Hawaii and Pennsylvania right-to-bargain and strike laws and the permissive New Hampshire legislation discussed earlier, negotiation statutes were passed in the early 1970s in Alaska, Idaho, Kansas, Montana, and Oklahoma. And teacher groups were working for legislation in many other states. By 1974 bargaining laws covering teachers were in force in 26 states, with four others having permissive bargaining allowing, if not requiring, school boards to meet with teachers. By 1972 a total of 1,445,329 instructional personnel throughout the nation were covered by negotiated agreements; in 1967 the number covered had been just 208,500.

Throughout the late 1960s and early 1970s affiliates of NEA bargained for the majority of teachers (nearly eight of every 10 teachers in school systems with agreements in the 1972–73 school year). But AFT too continued its efforts and by the 1972–73 school year was bargaining for 205,700 teachers in 128 school districts. This struggle between affiliates of NEA and of AFT to bargain for more teachers was just a part of the larger conflict between their national organizations.

11 / NEA and AFT:

To Fight or to Merge?

COMPETITION BETWEEN the National Education Association and the American Federation of Teachers, AFL-CIO, had gone on throughout the century. It was mostly desultory, however, until the 1960s, even though the union occasionally took it very seriously, nearly with paranoia. The capture of New York City teachers by an AFT local in 1961 sounded the bell for a new round of conflict. And in 1964 the competition sharpened. The union, now 18,311 members and 26 locals larger than it had been a year earlier, elected a new, more militant leader and expanded its drive to recruit teachers. The new president was Charles Cogen, former head of the New York City United Federation of Teachers. Defeating a conservative candidate who was an Indiana man handpicked by outgoing president Carl J. Megel, Cogen predicted he would lead AFT to a far more militant future. AFT launched a drive to get one dollar from every AFL-CIO member in the nation to support its organizing. In September, 1964, AFT announced that it had chosen target areas for intensive collective bargaining and organizing drives. Specifically mentioned were St. Louis, Boston, and Baltimore. In November Cogen announced a massive "Co-Org" (cooperative organizing) plan, "utilizing the resources of the national, state, and local AFT federations along with aid from the Industrial Union Department of the American Federation of Labor and Congress of Industrial Organizations." The plan attacked the problem in four steps, union spokesmen said: "1) State federations are being assisted to establish offices, organizing and servicing staffs and other important steps necessary to give proper representation for union teachers. 2) Smaller locals, in addition to receiving increased service through the expanded state federation programs, are being encouraged to join together in new 'area councils' to provide services closer to the point of impact than could normally be provided by state and national staffs. 3) Collective bargaining campaigns are receiving direct help from AFT headquarters. 4) Provision is made for meeting emergency situations as they arise throughout the year."

NEA, too, was fighting to win more teachers to its banner. Representing 903,384 members, delegates to the 1964 NEA convention approved a budget that increased funds for the union-fighting Urban Services Project for the third consecutive year. They okayed spending $442,000 on this unit, compared with the $389,235 spent the preceding year. Even more important, the NEA Board of Directors approved a recommendation that the executive secretary be authorized to spend up to a half million dollars from reserve funds to help local affiliates improve their programs and "maintain their professional independence"—in other words, fight off AFT challenges. Some of these funds were put to immediate use; by September, 1964, full-time executive secretaries were employed in 58 NEA urban affiliates. NEA and state association funds were often used to subsidize local affiliates that could not, at least initially, afford to hire full-time workers.

NEA expressed its concern about "independence of the profession" one other way in 1964. The Educational Policies Commission, a joint body of NEA and the American Association of School Administrators, issued a six-page brochure, "The Public Interest in How Teachers Organize," underlining the point that teachers must remain free from every other element in society:

> An organization of educators should have the following characteristics: It should perform many of the functions which contribute both to the betterment of the schools and to the welfare of the teachers; it should be organized independently; and it should promote the unity of teachers, administrators, and other educators. An organization which is consistent with these characteristics helps teachers to do their best for the pupils and for themselves. But organizations which are inconsistent with these characteristics diminish the effectiveness of teaching. That is why the way teachers organize is of great public importance.

1964 ELECTIONS

NEA and AFT affiliates, with help from their state and national parents, competed for control of teachers in six large cities in 1964. NEA affiliates won representation rights in three of the cities, AFT affiliates won in two, and one was a draw. NEA's victories were in Milwaukee, Wisconsin; Rochester, New York; and Newark, New Jersey. Milwaukee teachers went to the polls to choose an exclusive representative agent on February 11 and 12. The vote was 2,249 for the Milwaukee Teachers Education Association and 1,645 for the Milwaukee Teachers Union. NEA executive secretary William G. Carr, choosing a well-used phrase, termed the election victory a "significant turning point in American education." In a December 2 election the Rochester Teachers Association was selected representative for the teachers of that city with the NEA affiliate receiving 1,185 votes to the union's 692. The president of the winning Rochester group said the main campaign issue was the independence of the teaching profession versus teacher affiliation with organized labor. The third large-city victory for NEA in 1964 took place in Newark on December 15 in a close election. NEA's affiliate received 1,466 votes to 1,446 for the union, with 12 votes cast for neither. The election was a runoff of an earlier one which had ended with a 1,373 to 1,373 tie, and lawyers were contesting the second tally even as it was reported.

The American Federation of Teachers' big representation victories of 1964 occurred in Detroit and Cleveland. The Detroit election was won by the union May 11 by a three to two margin, 5,739 votes going to the federation and 3,848 going to the association. During the summer the federation negotiated a $50 increase in annual salaries for all teachers, with a second $50 increase due February, 1965. The June election in Cleveland was close and bitterly fought. Cleveland Education Association workers charged before the election that the school board had "knowingly stacked the deck in favor of the Cleveland Teachers Union" by excluding many certified personnel who were association members. The union won with 2,701 votes to the association's 2,026, with 162 teachers voting against both. The NEA-AFT draw occurred in Chicago, where the Teachers Union threatened to strike early in 1964 if the school board did not agree to negotiate with it. On February 27 the board approved a "collective bargaining memorandum" with the union. The union had wanted an agreement giving it exclusive bargaining rights, but it accepted the memorandum as a first step. Two weeks later the board approved a second collective bargaining memorandum, this time with the Chicago division of the Illinois Education Association. Each group was thus permitted to negotiate for its members.

Seven teachers' elections took place in smaller cities and towns during 1964, and NEA affiliates won most of them. On February 28 teachers voted 241 to 106 in favor of the Bremerton (Washington) Education Association. The election was called "doubly meaningful" by an NEA official "because these teachers have been represented by a union group since 1945. They have had an opportunity to see what a teachers' union can do, and as a result they have chosen to change to professional methods." On March 20 the teachers of New

Rochelle, New York, voted 317 to 274 for the NEA affiliate to represent them. On April 9 teachers chose the Jamesville (Wisconsin) Education Association over the union. On April 14 teachers in the Milwaukee suburbs, by a vote of 320 to 189, chose the West Allis-West Milwaukee Teachers Association. The South Kitsap (Washington) Education Association won over the local union by a vote of 161 to 88 on May 6. Some of the elections were indecisive. Twice in May, for example, teachers in Yonkers, New York, went to the polls to choose a representative. Both times, however, neither the association nor the union could get a majority of votes.

Representation campaigns were warming up in several other cities as 1964 ended, especially in two large ones: Boston and Philadelphia. The Boston Teachers Union (BTU) was demanding an election to choose a collective bargaining agent. There was no NEA affiliate in the city, most of whose teachers were members of the Boston Teachers Alliance, an old and independent group. NEA approached the alliance several times and tried to get it to affiliate with the national group and the Massachusetts Teachers Association, but to no avail. As 1964 ended, membership of the alliance and the union was in a nip-and-tuck range of 1,000 to 1,300 each. When about 70 percent of the teachers of Boston voted in an election on November 9, 1965, it was 1,602 for the union, 1,116 for the alliance. The union won by portraying itself as an activist group opposing the older, more conservative alliance. The union also apparently spent much more money in the campaign than did its opponent. A newspaper writer covering the election said, "With national financial support, the BTU offered both free coffee and free parking. It had posted three banners for voters to pass on the way to the polls. And it had reached each teacher with no less than six mailings the week before." In Philadelphia, both the Teachers Association (PTA) and the Federation of Teachers (PFT) sought an election throughout 1964. The association was certain it could win an early election, but its efforts to bring a ballot were slowed by a change of school superintendents. In early November the new superintendent asked the school board to authorize and direct him to present an election plan by December. The association, with guidance from NEA, the Pennsylvania State Education Association, and the nearby New Jersey Education Association, urged a January election; the union, wanting more time to overcome the years of domination by the association, asked for a March or April election. The date was set, in a compromise, for February 1, 1965. Both NEA and AFT spent money and sent in staff members to help their affiliates win the election. NEA's state affiliates in Pennsylvania and New Jersey also supplied workers and funds. The association lost by 732 votes—PFT 5,403, PTA 4,671. More than 95 percent of the teachers voted. For the union, the election was an emotional boost; for the associations, it was a cause for reexamination of goals and methods. Various reasons were put forth for the union's victory, but the consensus was that teachers had voted for change and against the lackluster record of the aging teachers association. A *Philadelphia Bulletin* analyst said: "For many years, it was generally understood that a good way to advance through the ranks into administration here was to take leadership in the PTA. All the key administrators belonged to it; many had been very active in their younger days. . . . But the AFT, in its campaign, kept hammering on the record of the old PTA leadership. It scored points as well, perhaps, on the civil rights issue. The NEA has segregated affiliates in the south which it is only now seeking to integrate." *Philadelphia Inquirer* writer Peter A. Janssen said that teacher morale was the key factor in the election. In their minds, teachers linked the PTA with the school administration and with the apathetic past. Janssen concluded: "During the campaign the federation successfully linked the association to the decline of the school system. Association campaigners tried to respond by stressing the 'new look' of their own leadership. . . . But the association's 'new look' at the top wasn't enough to overcome years of alleged passivity. The federation arraigned them and found them guilty

at least as co-partners in the sorry state of Philadelphia public
education. Mrs. Steet [the association president] gave this post
mortem of the election: 'We weren't fighting the union. It's
that obvious. We were fighting the low morale in the school
system.' "

1965 Elections

But the rivalry in 1965 for teacher representation went
beyond the big cities. Elections were also taking place in
smaller cities, towns, and rural districts. On January 28 teachers
in Tulsa, Oklahoma, voted 1,841 to 717 for representation by
the Tulsa Education Association. The Tulsa Federation of
Teachers withdrew from the balloting, concentrating instead on
encouraging votes against the association. A union vice-president said after the election, "This is a terrific achievement for
the federation in that we persuaded a third of the teachers to
stand with us in rejecting the proposal." On February 3 teachers
in Kenosha, Wisconsin, chose the teachers association as their
representative by a vote of 364 to 309 for the union. AFT locals
lost two 1965 elections by default—deciding not to expend
money and organizers on lost causes. In Racine, Wisconsin, on
April 8, teachers voted 700 to 15 for representation by the
Racine Education Association. And in New Haven, Connecticut, the NEA affiliate received 627 of 801 votes to become the
teachers' representative. AFT affiliates won spring elections in
Yonkers, New York; Mastic, New York; and Ashland, Wisconsin. The votes were 733 to 449 in Yonkers, 60 to 55 in
Mastic, 50 to 38 in Ashland.

Other AFT-NEA battlegrounds in 1965 were Connecticut,
Michigan, and Washington. Connecticut had a new law
mandating that school boards negotiate with teacher groups.
The law allowed school boards to recognize a teacher group
without an election if it was the only one in the district or if no
opposing group declared itself a candidate. By December 1,
1965, a total of 21 districts had officially designated local

affiliates of the Connecticut Education Association and NEA as the exclusive representative of the teachers. The law allowed a school board to hold representation elections if a negotiation agent could not be designated through common consent. In addition, the law allowed a school board to hold an election by its own choice regardless of whether one or more groups was trying to represent teachers in a district. If just one group was involved, then teachers would be allowed to vote for "no organization." Under this part of the law 22 elections were held between June 24 and the end of the year. Unions opposed associations in 17 elections. Of these 17, the union won a single election, in Hartford, where the vote was 527 to 498. NEA affiliates won the remaining 16 and also won five elections in which the union did not compete.

A teacher-school board negotiation law also passed in the state of Washington in 1965. It was in effect when the fall term began, and the Washington Education Association, which had sponsored the law, asked for elections in nearly every school district in the state. By November more than 40 districts had held elections. Spokane's election was typical. The union, having as members perhaps 2 percent of the staff, urged teachers to vote against the Spokane Education Association. The election was October 28, with 91.4 percent of the eligible staff members casting ballots. Of the 1,468 voting, 1,409 chose to be represented by the Spokane Education Association. The other Washington elections in 1965 were equally one-sided; in none of them did an AFT union even appear on the ballot. Michigan's elections in 1965, held under the state's labor law, were much the same story. During the fall, education associations won 10 of 14 elections and were stipulated as teacher representation agents in 105 additional districts.

During the mid-1960s a pattern was becoming clear: large cities for the unions and the rest of the nation for NEA. Affiliates of the AFT had won representation rights in two large cities: Philadelphia and Boston. Elsewhere, especially in the states of Connecticut, Washington, and Michigan, groups affiliated with the NEA were chosen in large numbers.

During this same period, election efforts were sometimes frustrated. Unions and associations challenged one another in four large cities without coming to the point of a representation election. In St. Louis, beginning late in 1964, both the association and the union talked about an election, but the state law clearly forbade school boards from signing collective bargaining agreements, so no election was held. In Detroit the local association, which had lost to the Detroit Federation of Teachers in May, 1964, decided not to contest for representation rights in 1965. In the 1964 election many Detroit Education Association members had been declared ineligible to vote because they were not classroom teachers; when the association was unable to obtain judicial relief in changing the election rules, it decided to bide its time. In Chicago, where union power was growing, an election and control by the union seemed inevitable by the fall of 1965. On September 12 the board of education voted six to two to hold an election to determine a sole bargaining agent for teachers. Both the Chicago Teachers Union and the Chicago Education Association had been recognized earlier as spokesmen for their own members. The association sued for an injunction to stop the board from holding an election, maintaining that the proposed contest was rigged in favor of the union. A series of court hearings delayed the election until 1966. When the clearly dominant Chicago Teachers Union received 10,936 votes in an election on May 27 and 28, NEA's affiliates gave up; the association had urged its members not to vote, and only 326 wrote in the association on the ballot. The fourth big-city challenge took place in Washington, D.C. The District of Columbia Education Association claimed 4,085 members from among the approximately 6,000 teachers in the system. Nevertheless, AFT national president Charles Cogen announced early in the fall that Washington, D.C., would be a prime union target. By the end of the year, the Teachers Union of Washington was hinting that it wanted a representation election while the association was demanding exclusive negotiation rights on the basis of petitions signed by 4,572 teachers. But the Washington school board refused to call an election or to grant recognition to any group.

AFT challenges to NEA affiliates in large cities may have left many other of its locals unserviced, for the AFT's 1965 membership gain was only 10,391, considerably less than the 18,311 gain of the preceding year. During the August, 1965, AFT convention, leaders reported that only 41 locals had met their membership quotas. The number of locals had increased, however, with 57 chartered between July, 1964, and May, 1965. AFT President Cogen, addressing the 1965 convention, assured members that numbers alone were not important. "Membership means nothing without program and a sense of mission, and the participation and involvement of all our members in what we are doing," he told union teachers. "If numbers were all that counted, the associations, with their huge captive memberships, would be invulnerable." In the same speech, Cogen attacked those associations, which, he said, continued to oppose genuine collective bargaining bills in the state legislatures and to substitute their own toothless imitations. "I know we are going to win this battle," he said. "We are going to win despite all their attempts to offer an imitation union as a substitute. We are going to win because we place the welfare of teachers first. We are not hobbled by the necessity of making sure that the managerial prerogatives of superintendents and principals are unimpaired. We are going to win because we firmly believe that teachers should be an integral part of organized society—not isolated from other organized employees."

AFT efforts to organize teachers in 1965 continued to receive the financial backing of the Industrial Union Department of the AFL-CIO. One report indicated that the department had committed $100,000 to the AFT drive in California alone. AFT's largest local, the United Federation of Teachers in New York City, had a strong year in 1965, beginning to speak for private school teachers in the city and for public school secretaries. Its biggest plum was a new contract giving New York City teachers the highest pay they had ever received. The contract, negotiated at the eleventh hour with the board of education, set top salaries at $11,950, well above the pay in any other large city in the country. The new contract also provided improved health insurance and a welfare fund, allowed preparation periods, and cut back on the teaching load. As in preceding years, UFT won the contract by a strike threat, this one lasting from June until September. The strike threat and the emergency nature of the negotiations led one observer, *New York Times* education writer Leonard Buder, to ask if collective bargaining between teachers and school boards could really work at all. Further, he asked, does collective bargaining help or hurt education? Arguing that collective bargaining in education is different and less supportable than in industry, he said that the procedure "threatens to destroy the budget-making powers of the education authorities and the integrity of the school system." His questions went unanswered in theory, but in practice the answers were to be written by the hundreds of school districts that would, increasingly, negotiate with the teacher groups in the future.

1966 ELECTIONS

When NEA's executive secretary spoke to convention delegates in 1966, he reported NEA affiliates had an excellent record in winning elections that determined the negotiating agent for teachers. Representation elections, or stipulations of exclusive representation without election, had taken place in five states up to June, 1966, and NEA affiliates were chosen in 200 districts, winning more than 87 percent of the elections. In California, where the law provided for negotiation councils based on proportional representation, association representatives won all nine council seats in San Francisco and San Diego. In Los Angeles the associations won eight of nine seats. This same pattern continued into 1967—of 62 elections between September 1, 1966, and June 16, 1967, NEA affiliates won 39 and AFT 23.

In one area of the rivalry—organizing college teachers— AFT got a head start on NEA. In April, 1966, AFT sponsored a nationwide conference designed "to fashion a program for teachers at institutions of higher education that would result in improved economic benefits, guarantees of academic freedom, and a genuine voice in decision making for faculty members." AFT said that its membership on college campuses had "zoomed up to 10,000 and that new locals are being chartered in record numbers at colleges and universities." NEA, in 1966, did not have a mechanism for negotiating for professors. Its Association for Higher Education, which enrolled about 20,000 professors and college administrators, did not attempt this role, for which it was soon to be ousted from the NEA family.

Overall, both NEA and AFT continued to grow in numbers. The union gained 14,899 members by mid-year 1966, giving it a total of 125,421. NEA grew from 943,581 to 986,113 during the 1965–66 school year, an increase of nearly 43,000 members. AFT also added 78 locals during the year, bringing the number of its active locals to 634.

As the number of representation elections increased, so did the claims and counterclaims of NEA and AFT. In February, 1966, AFT claimed that union teachers in the nation earned $831 more than their nonunion counterparts. NEA came back in April with a 15-page memorandum prepared by its research division. The memo concluded, "The evidence reviewed . . . leads to a rejection of the hypotheses that the mere existence of a teachers' union has the effect of pushing teachers' salaries upward. . . . Organized effort by the local, state, and national professional associations of teachers appears to be the most productive approach that teachers can take in seeking to improve the schools and raise the salaries of teachers." Yet in the midst of the often heated dispute between AFT and NEA came the first dialogue on possible merger of the two groups. At the 1966 NEA convention, NEA president Richard Batchelder publicly invited "our colleagues in the American Federation of Teachers to sever ties with labor and to unite with the National Education Association." It is doubtful that Batchelder expected any union members to leap at his invitation, but the AFT president did respond. Not surprisingly, he said that AFT affiliation with the AFL-CIO "has been of great benefit in pursuing the objective of improvements for the teaching profession" and that "we therefore have no intention of forsaking our affiliation with organized labor." Batchelder told the convention of the AFT response and poked considerable fun at it, to the enjoyment of the audience. So, as 1966 ended, the union and NEA moved their separate but often similar directions. The question of merger would officially arise again in two years; in the meantime, the organizations continued to compete.

BARGAINING IN 1967

From January through June, 1967, local affiliates of either AFT or NEA won bargaining rights in nine large cities. Although both crowed over their respective victories, within this six-month period AFT clearly made the larger gain as its affiliates emerged with firm negotiation rights in five of the nine cities: Cleveland, Detroit, Washington, D.C., Baltimore, and Chicago. In two of these cities—Washington and Baltimore—AFT even ousted the NEA affiliate for the first time. In contrast, NEA affiliates could claim only four victories during this period: in Denver, Jersey City, Milwaukee, and Buffalo. None of these cities were wrested from AFT control; on the contrary, in three of the cities, the NEA affiliate was maintaining control already established and in the fourth, Buffalo, was able to win by only a narrow margin. In January, 1967, the Cleveland Board of Education adopted procedures recognizing the Cleveland Teachers Union as the sole bargaining agent for the city's teachers. The board action climaxed a three-year struggle between the union and the Cleveland Education Association over which group was preferred by teachers. When balloting was finally scheduled in the winter of 1966, the association backed off, claiming the choice was predetermined by rules that favored the union. In view of this refusal, the board of education granted the union recognition rights by default. A few months later, March 29, NEA's affiliate in Denver grasped firmer control of negotiations in that city. The Denver Classroom Teachers Association had previously been selected by the city's teachers, and a negotiation agreement was in effect between the association and the school board. In 1967, however, the teachers were scheduled to vote again for their choice of a representative. Despite an intensive campaign by union teachers, who numbered about 500 among Denver teachers, the NEA affiliate was again picked, by a vote of 2,361 to 1,355. In April the AFT local in Detroit reaffirmed its control. By a vote of 6,410 to 3,709, the Detroit Federation Teachers defeated the Detroit Education Association. The election was a repetition, with a slight twist, of the 1964 contest, in which the federation originally was elected to represent the city's teachers. In the 1964 election, the association believed it had lost because it was considered a do-nothing organization. In 1967 it chose to claim it would be more militant than the union. This action, called "ill-tempered sniping" by one Detroit newspaper, did little good, for the federation received a greater percentage of the vote in 1967 than it had in 1964.

But it was in the Baltimore and Washington, D.C., elections that AFT worked hardest and involved a major share of its staff during 1967. And it won both. AFT's extensive help to local organizers in Washington included use of national representatives George Brickhouse, Joseph Cascella, Richard Hixson, Roger Kuh, Robert Crosier, and John Converse. James E. Munday, AFT director of organization, came in, as did state federation representatives like Charles Cheng of Michigan, Dick Bennett of Minnesota and Ken Miesen of Ohio and local union leaders like Arthur Brouillet and Anna Minelli of Hartford; Mary Riley of Minneapolis; Paul Devlin, Peabody, Massachusetts; Zeline Richard, Detroit; and Rollie Hopgood, Taylor, Michigan. Local leaders from other areas each came in for a few days just before the election; others devoted longer periods to the campaign. Albert Shanker, president of the United Federation of Teachers, New York City, and Mary Ellen Riordan, president of the Detroit Federation of Teachers, spoke at Washington rallies. It is likely that some of the organizers, if not the majority, worked in the Baltimore campaign as well, since that election was only six weeks after the Washington one.

The election in Washington was April 28, with the union receiving 3,540 votes to the association's 2,119. Shortly after the election, AFT announced that a referendum among its members had resulted in a four-to-three vote in favor of moving the union's national headquarters to Washington, D.C. The move was made in the fall of 1967.

For the Baltimore election, NEA chose to use the sanction and AFT the strike. An NEA report issued in April called Baltimore inner-city schools "dangerous"; it said its investigating team had found "teachers underpaid, buildings underequipped and undermaintained, the schools understaffed, and the school system underfinanced by the city." On July 8, NEA invoked sanctions against the Baltimore schools, the first time NEA national sanctions had been imposed on a city school system. Meanwhile, AFT called a strike. Nearly 300 teachers were arrested on picket lines May 11 and 12. Each group was generous with high-sounding rhetoric. NEA's report condemning the city schools was issued, the association said, because of its concern about working conditions there. AFT's strike was called, the union said, to gain assurance that teachers would have a chance to vote in a representation election. Neither group admitted that its actions were attempts to convince Baltimore teachers of their militancy. The teachers made their choice on June 16: AFT's local, the Baltimore Teachers Union, won over the Public School Teachers Association by a vote of 3,687 to 3,358. (The association would recapture the city seven years later, just in time to lead teachers on strike.)

NEA's affiliates won the three remaining representation elections in the spring of 1967. On May 3 the Jersey City Education Association was chosen by teachers over the Jersey City Federation of Teachers by a vote of 800 to 745. AFT said the NEA bargainers had won because they took credit for gains negotiated by the union, and it ridiculed what it called a "less-than-majority win." On June 1 Milwaukee teachers reasserted their preference for the Milwaukee Teachers Education Association by a vote of 2,258 to 1,477 for the AFT affiliate. And on June 6 Buffalo, New York, teachers gave 1,675 votes to the NEA affiliate, the Buffalo Teachers Federation. The American Federation of Teachers at Buffalo received 1,451 votes in the close contest.

AFT continued its efforts to organize college teachers in 1967. It had nearly 15,000 college and university professors on its membership rolls, won a couple of successful college strikes, and scored several collective bargaining victories. NEA countered by chartering its National Faculty Association of Community and Junior Colleges in Washington, D.C., on May 28, 1967. The group began trying to organize chapters on college campuses, much as the AFT had been doing for several years.

Both AFT and NEA grew in membership during 1967. AFT reported by April that its membership topped 136,000; by summer it officially hit 142,012. The union also added 55 new locals during the year. In 1967 NEA membership topped one million for the first time in the history of the association. The million mark was passed in March, 1967, and the 1966–67 school year total membership was 1,028,456. NEA membership growth in one year had been 42,343; AFT growth during the same period was 16,591. At this point, labor columnist Victor

Riesel commented on the NEA-AFT struggle. In a column published during the fall of 1967, he said:

The real issue . . . is blackboard power among the teachers of the land. Fact is that the AFL-CIO teachers union—despite all the hubbub and brick pounding—has not done so well in academic circles. Back about 1960, the AFT had some 50,000 members. Then came Walter Reuther and his AFL-CIO Industrial Union Department. They sent in organizers. They put a steady staff into New York. They revamped the AFT's Chicago office. They put militant little Charley Cogen in a bright new saddle. Since 1961, they have poured in $1.1 million. They did right well in New York, where it is impossible not to do well on the labor front. They enrolled some 49,000 members. And when they had the original membership and the newcomers all totaled up across the land, they found they had 140,000 dues payers. And the AFT totaled its contracts and found the other day that it has pacts in 41 school districts. Not much compared with the 1,336 exclusive NEA contracts covering 650,000 certificated teachers in 45 states. Thus the so-called militant teachers who are now striking regularly under the AFT leadership have 3 percent of the exclusive bargaining contracts compared with the 93.7 percent negotiated by the 100-year-old NEA. The so-called old lady of the teaching business turns out to be a mighty spry chick. It has not gone to pot with flower power. When the AFT teachers began moving, there was parallel NEA action. The Washington-based association—housed in a big block-long structure and employing about 1,000 staffers—began collective bargaining five years ago. These pacts are negotiated by officials of the NEA's 8,000 local affiliates in 50 states.

COMPETITION IN 1968

The NEA-AFT competition continued into 1968 when the AFT won representation rights over NEA affiliates in four additional large cities: Pittsburgh, Toledo, Kansas City, Missouri, and Wilmington, Delaware. Further, AFT affiliates reaffirmed their control over Cleveland and won a majority of seats on negotiating councils in Minneapolis and St. Paul. The

Pittsburgh election was close: On April 24 the Pittsburgh Teachers Education Association captured 22 more votes than did the Pittsburgh Federation of Teachers, the AFT local. But neither organization received a majority of votes, and a runoff election was May 23. The AFT affiliate won that election by a vote of 1,772 to 1,590. The Pittsburgh Federation claimed the main difference between the elections was that the second election balloting was held outside administrative offices, where teachers could not be observed by their bosses. Also in May, the AFT affiliate in Toledo defeated the NEA affiliate by a vote of 1,217 to 966. The election was hailed by AFT as a "major reversal for company-unionism in the United States"; the Toledo Education Association had won a 1966 election there.

The Kansas City Federation of Teachers won representation rights on June 6 by a vote of 1,317 to 1,100. The NEA affiliate, the Kansas City Education Association, claimed a telegram purporting to be from black civil rights leader Ralph David Abernathy was fraudulently used in the last days of the campaign, but nothing came of the charge and the AFT affiliate began negotiating with the Kansas City school board. In December AFT won its fourth major city of the year when an election gave the Wilmington [Delaware] Federation of Teachers representation rights by a vote of 417 to 325. AFT reaffirmed its control in Cleveland when its local, the Cleveland Teachers Union, won a four-to-one majority of ballots cast by teachers in January. The vote was 4,105½ for the union, 1,413½ for the Cleveland Education Association. Under Minnesota law the school board in Minneapolis and St. Paul could name representatives to negotiating councils based on declarations of membership. On October 15, the deadline for reporting membership, AFT locals in both cities exceeded the membership of the NEA affiliates. As a result, the unions were given the majority of seats on the five-man councils.

Affiliates of NEA did not come up empty-handed in 1968 elections, however. On January 31 the NEA affiliate in Cincinnati received 2,019 votes to the Cincinnati Teachers Union's

530 and was named sole bargaining agent. Two days before the election, about 700 union teachers went on strike in an attempt to demonstrate the union's militancy. But when a judge issued an injunction ordering them back into the classrooms, the strike collapsed. In March the NEA affiliate in San Francisco won a majority of votes and the right to negotiate for teachers. The NEA group got 51 percent of the vote, the union 44 percent. The NEA affiliate in nearby Oakland also won a majority of seats on its negotiating council. As a result, an NEA spokesman said affiliates of NEA had "virtually shut the West Coast door" on the hopes of AFT to recruit teachers. An NEA affiliate also won control of negotiation in Dade County, Florida, which encompasses Miami and Miami Beach. On November 21, the school board voted to recognize the Dade County Classroom Teachers Association as the sole negotiating agent for the system's professional staff. Both the union and an independent teachers group objected to the ruling, but court efforts to overturn it were unsuccessful.

Despite the continuing challenges in the large cities, NEA's overall membership grew by 53,204 in 1968 to hit a total of 1,081,660, the second consecutive year of more than one million members. The association also increased the number of its affiliates by 379, bringing them to a record total of 8,643. In addition, NEA continued to press its drive to bring unified membership into more and more states. Under this plan all members of a state education association must also join NEA. Thirty state associations were committed to unification by the fall of 1968. Five additional large states—California, Maryland, New York, Texas, and Wisconsin—took steps toward unification before the year ended.

The American Federation of Teachers, too, enjoyed a record membership gain in 1968 by adding 21,326 members to bring its total membership to 154,956. AFT also made a net gain of 64 locals, adding 104 and losing 40 that became inactive during the year. Two of the union's locals activated during the 1967–68 school year represented parochial school teachers. In

159

February the teachers in the Catholic archdiocesan high schools in Philadelphia became AFT local 1776; earlier, Hebrew teachers in Los Angeles had voted to affiliate with AFT. But despite its growth during 1968, AFT was being caught in a financial squeeze. Early in 1968 Walter Reuther, then leader of the United Auto Workers and a vice president of the AFL-CIO, began seeking labor friends who would split with him from the main labor body. Later in the year, Reuther refused to pay dues to the AFL-CIO, and later still he withdrew from UAW to form a new labor group, the Alliance for Labor Action. This split within the labor movement was costly to AFT, which had received an estimated $5 million to $6 million from the Reuther-led Industrial Union Department of the AFL-CIO. Without this subsidy, AFT was not financially stable; it was more than $275,000 in debt. According to its financial statement of June 30, 1968, its "accounts payable" stood at $230,000 and its outstanding "expansion fund" debentures totaled $255,000. No lists of the accounts of the debenture holders were published in the statement. Certificates of indebtedness came to $64,000. To offset this deficit, the AFT leadership proposed an increase in the per capita dues that each local paid to the national federation. The increase was approved by the convention, but only after extensive debate and a challenge led by Albert Shanker, president of the New York City UFT, who emphasized that the national union was going into debt at a rate of $35,000 a month. AFT delegates finally passed the dues increase in a close vote, 1,096 to 1,082.

Call for Merger

Partly because of its weak financial position, AFT began in 1968 to call again for a merger with NEA. David Selden, newly elected AFT president, said that merger of the two groups was "the overriding goal of my administration." He explained: "Among teachers there is a vast yearning for unity. In unity there is strength, and the teachers are aware of their powerlessness. They want more power—power to change the present educational system. . . . The greatest deterrent to militancy is the belief that one cannot win. A unified organization is apt to be more militant than either organization now has the power to be." On October 4, 1968, Selden sent a letter to NEA President Elizabeth D. Koontz. Its first paragraph said: "Bringing together teachers in one unified powerful organization is the most important task confronting leaders of the profession today. A high-ranking committee of the American Federation of Teachers is eager to meet with representatives of the National Education Association to discuss this problem. We advance this suggestion without preconditions of any kind. We hope that you will find it possible to respond favorably." Selden sent a similar letter to the president of the NEA's Association of Classroom Teachers. At the same time, he called a press conference at which he announced seven "tentative proposals" for the merged group he envisaged: 1) Sovereignty of the teaching profession would be established. 2) NEA would be broadened to include all pro-education groups. 3) Memberships would be through locals chartered by the national organization. 4) Local and state organizations would have to conform to fair standards. 5) The new organization would promote collective bargaining. 6) The new organization would seek state and national agreements on basic conditions and school funds. 7) A national teacher defense and strike fund would be established.

NEA's response to Selden's proposals was rapid and negative. A telegram to Selden from Mrs. Koontz said: "The Executive Committee of the National Education Association declines your invitation of October 4 to meet to discuss 'one unified organization.' The concept of merger, which you have suggested publicly, assumes an organizational advantage for the parties concerned. We see no evidence of advantage to our teachers in your proposal." In explanation of the action, Mrs. Koontz alluded to the financial problems of AFT. She also referred to conflict among AFT officers and staff. Further, she said, there were indications of disenchantment in the ranks of

AFT, and some of its members had been seeking to join NEA. Shortly after this, the NEA Association of Classroom Teachers also rejected the union bid, vigorously applauding the NEA position.

Before the year was out, though, it became clear that NEA was sending AFT a message slightly different from an absolute rejection of merger. In December, 1968, an NEA official statement further explained the rejection of the AFT bid, reiterating the reasons given by President Koontz and adding that NEA had its own plan for unity; that is, unification of all local, state, and national education associations. But the statement's last paragraph added: "NEA is looking forward to the day when all teachers will be united in one comprehensive organization. Union members are welcome and urged to join the ranks of NEA and its state and local affiliates. If a combining of forces is to be achieved, it would be wise to begin at the local or state levels rather than attempt to merge from the top down. This plan offers the best hope for real unity among teachers." As the year ended, it was not clear whether NEA's apparent message—that merger must begin locally—had been heard by the AFT leadership. In mid-December, an Ohio Education Association official reiterated that "such cooperation will have to come from the local level." AFT published the comment in a news story in its official publication, but made no editorial comment. An area of possible common ground for merger now existed. A method was available for eventual unification of the teachers of the nation, a merger that could affect teacher militancy and change competitors into co-workers for the teachers' cause. But the merger did not come in the late 1960s, nor in the early 1970s. Instead, the rivalry grew.

THE FIGHT CONTINUES

Early in 1969, some 80 NEA leaders—classroom teachers, officers, and staff of state and local NEA affiliates—met in Washington, D.C., and decided to move ahead with an all-out push for a stronger association network around the nation. They called for NEA and its state affiliates to pay for staff help for local associations, for leadership training programs for state and local staff, for expansion of NEA economic services for members (such as insurance), for greater staffing of NEA's 11 regional offices, and for launching a fund of millions of dollars to help affiliates in trouble. They also agreed on $25 yearly NEA dues to finance these steps. This leadership plan was implemented within two years. NEA delegates to the 1969 Representative Assembly approved the higher dues; a program called UniServ was established to place one trained staff person locally for every 1,200 teachers in the nation; an NEA Leadership Training Academy was set up, with responsibility for training UniServ representatives set as a major priority; NEA staff, especially in regional offices, was expanded; and additional economic services were made available to NEA members.

The new thrust paid off; few members were lost in the raising of dues, with NEA membership remaining greater than one million in 1969. (It dropped to 1,014,414 in 1969, but the loss was more than made up in 1970, when it climbed 77,000 to nearly 1,100,000.) The UniServ program was pushed at first mainly in the unified-dues states, but within a few years more than 700 local staff workers had been employed; by 1974, about 900 UniServ representatives were at work. AFT membership, meanwhile, remained relatively low, increasing from 163,338 in 1968 to 170,694 in 1969. Nor would it gain substantially more members until the New York statewide teacher-group merger in 1972.

Representation election fights between NEA affiliates and AFT locals continued. More than 80 elections were held each year from 1969 through 1973. Typical was the 1972–73 school year. During that period, NEA won 56 representation elections; AFT won 19. Most of these elections were in urban school districts—Portland, Oregon; Houston; Watertown, Connecticut; Wilmington, Delaware; St. Paul—but more and more were on college campuses. Working through the National Higher Education Association and its units (the National Society of Professors, the National Faculty Association of Community and Junior Colleges, and the National Association of College and University Administrators), NEA was beginning in earnest to organize college faculty. During the 1969–70 school year, about 100 new chapters affiliated with the National Faculty Association of Community and Junior Colleges. And early in 1970 NEA's drive to organize college teachers bore additional fruit in two states, Michigan and New York. The Central Michigan University Chapter of the Michigan Association for Higher Education and the National Society of Professors negotiated NEA's first contract by a four-year college affiliate. The professors won pay raises averaging 12 percent and a faculty role in planning contracts. In New York, the faculty of one of the largest and most comprehensive education complexes in the nation, the City University of New York, voted to affiliate with NEA and the New York State Teachers Association. The faculty affiliated through their Legislative Conference, the recognized bargaining agent for 6,500 CUNY staff. AFT continued to recruit college teachers, as did the American Association of University Professors. During this same 1972–73 period, for example, AFT college locals won elections at the University of Hawaii, among New Jersey State Colleges, and at Northland College in Wisconsin. NEA faculty groups won at Loretto Heights College, Colorado; Ferris State College, Michigan; Westmoreland Community College, Pennsylvania; Roger Williams College, Rhode Island; and the Edmonds-Everett Community Colleges, Washington. AAUP was named bargaining agent on three campuses: Regis College in Colorado and Lincoln and Temple Universities in Pennsylvania. Several other campus representation struggles were draws, usually because the faculty voted for "no representation."

The idea of organizing—"unionizing"—college faculty was still relatively new. By October, 1972, the Academy of Educational Development (AED) reported that faculty unionization (which it opposed) had spread to 120 of the nation's four-year colleges and 147 two-year institutions (out of more than 2,000 colleges and universities). AED, estimating that about 10 percent of college professors were organized, was alarmed that in the collective bargaining process faculty unions might displace what it called "other important processes of a college-wide scope." And it expressed a concern similar to that noted by many public school superintendents: Where do you draw the line between clearly negotiable items—salary, work load, tenure, *et al.*—and questions of basic education policy—educational objectives, curriculum, or student evaluation? "It surely will not be easy to separate the two," AED concluded. By the end of 1973 the number of organized college faculties had grown to 314, and the pace of the college organizing drive continued. One side effect was the pressure some faculties put on college administrations to give them more power in college senates and other aspects of college governance. Presumably some administrators were acceding to these requests because they saw them as less dangerous than all-out unionization of faculty.

Meanwhile, negotiation agreements in public school districts continued to increase. By 1972 teachers covered by agreements numbered 1,445,329. The number of school systems with negotiation agreements increased to 3,911. In the battle of numbers in this negotiation game, NEA far outpaced AFT. Of the 3,911 systems covered by agreements, 3,891 were organized by NEA and its affiliates, just 126 by AFT.

AGAIN, PRESSURE FOR MERGER

AFT, by the end of 1972, was in a dilemma. Its growth spurt, started by the New York City victory in 1961, had ended. After capturing the allegiance of many big-city teachers (Philadelphia, Boston, and Cleveland, as examples), and after solidifying its membership base in some suburban areas with strong labor histories such as East St. Louis, AFT had nowhere to turn. It could spend organizing funds to confront NEA affiliates in cities and suburbs already firmly in association hands, but the rewards were not promising. Thousands of dollars were sometimes spent in vain, sometimes year after year, only to have the city revert to association control (Portland, Oregon, for example). Where to turn? Some union leaders in 1972 began again to look longingly at the idea of merger with NEA affiliates. Merger, they reasoned, would at least give them more members, even if the members had to be shared with NEA. Within the AFT leadership, David Selden (national president) and Albert Shanker (New York City president) started pushing the merger idea from slightly different angles. Selden began feeling out NEA leaders for national merger talks. Shanker, on the other hand, moved to unify all New York state teachers. Shanker's thought processes were not too hard to read: If Selden led a national merger, Shanker would remain big man in a relatively smaller New York pond; but if Shanker could pull off a statewide merger in New York, have himself chosen spokesman for that group of nearly 200,000 teachers, he would outflank Selden, represent the majority of AFT teachers in the nation, and eventually replace Selden as national AFT president as well. So in 1972, the die was cast as the two AFT leaders began working on merger. Their struggle, it would turn out, was to end without compromise, and also without merger.

Within the NEA, too, were some who favored merger: Thomas Hobart, a New York state teacher leader, and Donald Morrison, a San Diego teacher who was 1971–72 president. Others were Richard Batchelder, a former NEA president who was executive director of the Los Angeles teachers, later head of the Florida state NEA affiliate (and head of the Florida AFT group); and Pat Tornillo, executive director of the Dade County (Florida) Classroom Teachers Association and a leader in the National Council of Urban Education Associations. The motives of these individuals differed, as did the intensity of their belief in merger. Morrison smiled on merger talks while president of NEA, but respected the NEA Executive Committee's general disapproval of merger; he all but disappeared from merger discussions after his term ended. Batchelder first moved to become head of all California teachers through an NEA push for unification of membership in the state. When this failed, he merged his affiliate in Los Angeles with the teacher union there. In Florida, he backed Tornillo in a merger of Dade County teachers and later pressed a statewide merger.

In New York state, where Shanker was calling the shots, merger went quite smoothly at first. Inundated with talk of unity, impressed with the idea of facing the state legislature with a commonality of purpose, New York State Teachers Association leaders found themselves slowly won over to the idea of a tentative, loose merger with Shanker's 65,000 New York City teachers. In 1972 the merger in New York was pulled off, and a new state organization, the New York State United Teachers (NYSUT), was organized with Shanker and Hobart as its leaders. The new group compromised on NEA and AFT membership, allowing New York teachers the privilege of paying dues to both. Thus, NYSUT was dually an affiliate of NEA and, through AFT, an AFL-CIO union. (Earlier mergers —in Los Angeles and in Flint, Michigan, for example—had allowed teachers to pay dues to one or the other national group or to both if they wished.)

Some within NEA's leadership consistently opposed the merger. Typical of these was Sam M. Lambert, NEA executive secretary until early 1973. At the 1972 NEA convention Lambert told delegates of his fears about the New York merger and about merger in general. His prediction, which came true in less than two years, was that the New York merger was a stepping-stone for Albert Shanker to take over leadership within the state and within the AFT. "One-man control of the teachers of New York is inevitable," Lambert said. He also pointed out that to allow mergers such as the New York one to stand was to invite more and more mergers. "How many AFL-CIO states will you accommodate in the organization?" he asked the convention delegates. Finally, he wondered, "Will unity in New York mean disunity in NEA?" Statistics compiled by the NEA research division backed Lambert's concern: When polled on the merger question, 61 percent of NEA members said in 1972 that they would discontinue their membership if the national organization affiliated with AFL-CIO.

Lambert did not survive within NEA to see his words proven because he stepped down as executive secretary soon after the 1972 speech, but his warning was heeded. The 1972 NEA Representative Assembly passed Business Item #20, which stated, "In the future, the NEA and its affiliates will not enter into a merger requiring affiliation with the AFL-CIO." Item #20 grandfathered in New York and a few other local NEA affiliates that had already signed merger agreements, but it strengthened its intent by adding a paragraph of NEA support for the newly formed Coalition of American Public Employees. This group, led by NEA and the American Federation of State, County, and Municipal Employees (AFL-CIO), was disliked by AFT leaders, who saw it as a way of providing teachers the support of labor without requiring union dues. Head of the group and father of the coalition was AFSCME President Jerry Wurf, a man often at odds with Shanker.

At the 1973 NEA convention, Shanker, Hobart, and other New Yorkers—with votes from some Florida and California delegates—tried again to get approval of mergers between NEA and AFL-CIO affiliates. Failing this, they settled for a compromise: an action allowing national merger talks between NEA and AFT leaders, with a moratorium on local and state NEA-AFT competition during the talks. As passed, the 1973 NEA position included three major points: Any new organization formed by a merger would have to be outside the AFL-CIO; the new organization would have to accept the NEA commitment to guarantees or quotas for ethnic minority members; and the new organization would have to use the secret ballot for elections and other decision making. (AFT, like many labor groups, used an open-ballot, party-caucus voting method.) The majority of delegates to the 1973 NEA meeting opposed both Shanker and merger. But they accepted the leadership proposal to allow talks on merger as long as AFL-CIO membership was clearly out of the question. As a result, the fall and winter of 1973–74 was a time of great optimism for merger proponents. "Merger by Christmas," Selden told newsmen at the NEA convention in July, though he later admitted this might not be possible. NEA President Helen Wise promised that talks with AFT would begin as soon as practicable after September 1.

MERGER TALKS

So the merger talks between NEA and AFT leaders, long anticipated by observers of the education scene, actually took place between October, 1973, and February, 1974. Each group named a team to attend the talks. On the AFT side of the table were veterans Selden and Shanker. On the NEA side were all new faces. Pro-merger Presidents Batchelder and Morrison were long out of NEA office. Acting NEA executive secretary Allan West, who was at least neutral on the subject, had been replaced by a new, young teacher-leader, Terry Herndon. NEA President Wise was from Pennsylvania, a state unsympathetic to merger.

Though mildly optimistic reports on the merger talks were released as the two groups met, in actuality the 1.5 million NEA members and the 300,000 AFT members were never close to becoming one national group. At least three factors prevented agreement. First, the AFT leadership was engaging in a bloody internecine war. Shanker, as an AFT vice-president and with support from AFL-CIO boss George Meany, had been placed on the AFL-CIO executive council, bypassing AFT President Selden. Shanker then had announced that he would run for the AFT presidency in July, 1974. Finally, Shanker had asked that Selden step aside immediately in the interest of unity. Selden refused, after some days of debate with himself. Shanker then cut Selden's power by forming a committee of the AFT executive committee to review Selden's actions. Meanwhile, Shanker accused Selden of selling out to NEA in the talks by making secret offers to withdraw AFT from the AFL-CIO. In the midst of this warfare, NEA's representatives at the merger talks were unsure of how much meaning and strength were behind the AFT team led, ostensibly, by Selden. A second factor which limited success of the talks was the new NEA leadership. Terry Herndon became NEA executive secretary in the spring of 1973 when he was 34 years old. A quietly competent leader, he had plans for NEA's future, plans unlikely to include placing so aggressive a leader as Albert Shanker next to him in the executive suite, as would happen once a merger took place. NEA President Wise, too, had motives for maintaining an independent NEA. She was considering running for NEA president again in two years when, thanks to a change in the NEA constitution, presidents could serve longer terms. Thus NEA's top representatives at the table had little to gain from a merger. The final and central reason for the failure of the merger talks was AFT's intransigence on the matter of AFL-CIO membership. Despite a so-called compromise offered by Selden, the teacher-leaders never had before them a reasonable plan, or even the beginnings of a plan, that could have led to a national teacher merger outside the AFL-CIO. Both sides recognized from the beginning of the talks that AFL-CIO membership was the major issue, so they agreed to discuss that first, saying, in effect, that if the AFL-CIO affiliation issue could not be resolved, the talks could not succeed. And it could not be resolved. Selden's compromise consisted of the idea that the nation's teachers would all join in one group affiliated with the AFL-CIO, but that any teacher who didn't want his dues money used to pay AFL-CIO per capita fees could indicate his desire in writing. The NEA leaders pointed out that they could counter with a proposal that all teachers join in the national organization not affiliated with the AFL-CIO and then every teacher who wanted his dues paid on per capita basis to AFL-CIO could indicate so. Such a counterproposal seemed fruitless to NEA, so the talks ended February 28, 1974.

MERGER FAILURE

Each side blamed the other for the breakdown of the talks. In a February 28 press release, NEA said, "NEA wants teacher unity; AFT wants AFL-CIO membership. The two are not compatible." AFT President Selden called a press conference the following day and blamed the breakoff on the "unwillingness of the NEA to attempt to work out the problems which separate the two organizations." He said NEA's breaking off the talks was an irresponsible action. Shanker, in a *New York Times* advertisement March 3, 1974, said that NEA had shattered the hopes of teachers all across the country when it broke off the talks. He reiterated the values of AFL-CIO membership to teachers and suggested that teachers let NEA know how they felt by voting for AFT representation around the nation. But he, too, admitted that the merger idea was dead for some time. He said a merger might take place "in this decade," and he changed his announced strategy for merger. NEA will come around only when AFT becomes stronger, he now asserted, and he set target areas—Florida, California, Puerto Rico, and all of higher education—for organizing pushes. When AFT captures a few more states and a few hundred thousand more members, NEA will be willing to talk about meaningful merger, Shanker said.

Florida became the first testing ground for the new strategy. Through a series of steps, the NEA affiliate, the Florida Education Association, was moved from approving county and local mergers, to declaring itself independent, to merging with the AFT as "Florida Education Association/ United." NEA disaffiliated the group and established a new affiliate, first called Florida United Service Association, then the Florida Teaching Profession. By the winter of 1974, FEA/ United and the new NEA affiliate both had built their strongholds—the union's mainly in Pat Tornillo's Dade County and in Hillsborough County, the association's mainly in Brevard, Broward, and Leon Counties—and the fight was on.

Florida's legislature had passed a statewide public employee bargaining law; it went into effect January 1, 1975. Under this law, teacher groups could file for representation elections in each county. By mid-1975, elections were held in about ten counties. As a result, it seemed that the new NEA affiliate would represent a majority of Sunshine State teachers, claiming by June that it represented 42,000 of the 55,000 school staff in the state. The AFT group claimed about 35,000 teachers in its camp. To an extent, it was a stand-off.

Meanwhile, NEA-AFT conflict flared up in New York, the one fully merged state. Early in 1975, the NEA Board of Directors censured the leadership of the New York State United Teachers (NYSUT) for presenting "a distorted picture of the policies and positions of the National Education Association to the teachers of New York." Their publications failed to inform the state's teachers about the advantages of NEA membership, while at the same time promoting the interests and image of the American Federation of Teachers, the board said.

When NEA President James Harris spoke at the NYSUT annual meeting in March, he reiterated the charge, but tried to soften the blow, saying, "Talk about dissaffiliation is shortsighted, bordering on the irresponsible." He added that he was calling for NEA-NYSUT leadership meetings to work on the conflict. Several meetings were held, but to little avail. In the winter of 1975, NEA announced a "NEA in New York" project designed to strengthen its hand in the Empire State. NYSUT leaders immediately denounced the project as "outside interference" and as a step toward the establishment of a new pro-NEA, anti-AFT affiliate in the state. NEA's new president, John Ryor, told NYSUT leaders that NEA "very much wants

New York teachers to remain part of NEA," but NYSUT officials were unmoved. On November 22, 1975, the NYSUT board of directors voted 52 to 6 for a resolution that would delete all mention of NEA from the state group's constitution. Separation of NYSUT from NEA seemed inevitable.

NEA's president said he hoped NYSUT would not take final disaffiliation action, but he added that, whatever happened, NEA intended to "remain a presence in New York state."

With the New York split, hopes of NEA-AFT merger evaporated. America's teacher organizations entered the Bicentennial year farther from merger than ever.

12 / Social Issues
and Teacher Rights

TEACHERS EXPRESSED THEIR MILITANCY, especially in the 1960s and 1970s, through strikes and by winning contract agreements. They also became involved in social issues by taking sides in noneducational matters. They began to organize for political action. And they pursued their legal rights much more vigorously.

For decades both AFT and NEA had passed resolutions at their annual conventions, most of them relating directly to education and urging improved teaching conditions, higher salaries, better use of testing in the schools, and the like. During the 1960s and 1970s both groups expanded their resolutions to include noneducational social issues. Two examples of such AFT action illustrate this, and one of the examples gives another view of the Selden-Shanker conflict. In this latter case, the issue was whether the union would endorse a candidate for U.S. President in 1972. More specifically, the question was whether AFT would back Sen. George McGovern, since little support existed among its members for Richard Nixon. Normally, support for a candidate would be routinely declared by an AFT convention, funds would be raised, and publicity from AFT would urge teacher-members to vote for the candidate. But one factor was not normal in 1972: AFL-CIO President George Meany had ruled that labor would sit out the election —a decision obviously helpful to Nixon since labor support and money usually went to the liberal candidate; Meany's decision could hurt only McGovern. AFT President Selden, a man with a long history of liberalism, favored McGovern and wanted support for him. Albert Shanker normally would also have supported McGovern, for Shanker's record of liberalism was well known. He came from a classically liberal New York Jewish family and certainly was not a typical Nixon supporter. Shanker, however, wanted and needed Meany's support; and to maintain that support he had to try to manuever the AFT convention away from support for McGovern. To do so, he used his influence with the AFT delegates to promote a motion calling for a membership-wide canvass on endorsing a candidate. It seemed a fair idea except that it was already August; the survey of AFT members would take months, delaying canvass results until after the November election. The delegates voted down the Shanker proposal, 679 to 323, but George Meany could see that Shanker was on his side.

Another example of AFT social action was its support of the boycott of Farah products. Farah, a U.S. slacks manufacturer near the Mexican border, resisted union organizing for years. By 1970 unions throughout the AFL-CIO were calling for a boycott of Farah products. AFT supported the boycott, collected funds to support the families of displaced Farah workers, and publicized the charges of unfair labor practices against the company. The battle ended in 1974 when a federal court ordered the unionizing of the plants, ruling that Farah had indeed been guilty of unfair activities.

NEA support for noneducational issues occurred infrequently before 1969. Although NEA spoke out in general terms against business interests, especially during the depression, and in support of the war effort during World War II, most matters not directly related to education failed to win support from delegates to NEA's Representative Assemblies. Illustrative were the attempts by supporters of gun control to win NEA backing. For several consecutive years during the 1960s, NEA delegates favoring gun control placed a resolution or business item on this matter before the convention. Invariably, the item was defeated. What happened, in terms of the dynamics of parliamentary action, was this: supporters of the gun control measure would speak strongly for it. The opponents, usually from the northwestern states where hunting was a major industry and a way of life, spoke against it. Presumably each side won numerous hearts and votes. But inevitably some delegate, tired of the debate (or, craftily, opposed to the item) would rise to express the opinion that the matter, interesting as it was, was not an educational issue. "We are here to solve the schools' problems, not all the problems of society," the delegate would say. A motion to close debate would follow, and the vote would be taken. The gun control advocates usually got 30 percent of the vote; those opposed to gun control got an equal number. Added to the vote against, however, was the 40 percent of the delegates who didn't care strongly about the issue, but who were convinced it was not a matter for educators to decide. And the measure would go down in defeat. (Finally, in 1974, a gun control measure was approved by NEA delegates.) This predilection of NEA delegates to avoid non-educational issues drove to defeat motions supporting or opposing peace, the war in Southeast Asia, liberalization of drug laws, and other issues throughout the 1960s.

In the early 1970s, however, resolutions opposing President Nixon, who had vetoed school funding legislation, and favoring lessened penalties for drug offenders (teachers being close to the young people using these drugs) did pass the NEA Representative Assembly. But the strongest NEA social forays took place in 1969 and 1970 when the association's executive committee and board of directors spoke out several times on issues not directly related to schools. At the time President

Nixon had proposed for the Supreme Court judges Clement F. Haynsworth, Jr., and G. Harrold Carswell. NEA leadership groups voted to oppose these appointments and directed its staff to publicize this opposition. The result was an outpouring of letters from members attacking the idea that the NEA president or an elected panel of the association should speak for the membership. The same membership reaction followed in 1972, 1973, and 1974 when NEA presidents and committees spoke out against the Nixon administration's cuts in school funds and against the Watergate climate. The members who made these complaints had a point, but NEA officials were on firmer ground by then because NEA Representative Assemblies were voting opposition to the Nixon administration.

POLITICAL ACTION

As noted above, AFT ran into trouble attempting to endorse a political candidate in 1972. But its problem that year was not typical; AFT usually voted to support a national candidate. By 1974 NEA never had gone that far. But in the 1970s the association and its affiliates did begin to organize Political Action Committees (PACs) as mechanisms, both to support individual candidates and to collect funds to help elect them. By the end of 1972 committees were organized in 45 states; by 1974 PACs were at work in every state as well as nationally through an NEA-PAC. In February, 1974, NEA and its affiliates launched a drive to collect $1 a member for political action during the year. The association apportioned the money, hundreds of thousands of dollars, among pro-education candidates throughout the nation in the spring primaries and the fall election. NEA also began to publish the voting records of every U.S. Representative and Senator, showing its members the Congressmen's votes—wrong or right according to NEA—on major educational issues. The association's 1.5 million-circulation newspaper, the NEA Reporter, carried this voting record in 1972 and in 1974. And, at its 1974 annual

177

meeting, the national association set up a mechanism for endorsing a Presidential candidate in 1976.

TEACHER RIGHTS

But by far the greatest growth of teacher militancy outside of the traditional negotiation arena during this time was the fight for legal rights for teachers through court cases. Although many local and state unions and associations took part in this struggle, in most cases the defense of teacher rights depended upon financial and legal aid—from NEA or AFT.

Starting in the late 1940s, NEA had provided legal assistance to teachers under fire by school boards or the public. The association created the National Commission for the Defense of Democracy Through Education in 1941. Advocated by then NEA President Donald DuShane, the Defense Commission, as it was commonly called, was designed to become "a protagonist of schools, the defender of teachers, the upholder of academic freedom, and the castigator of unfriendly critics and avowed enemies of public education."

This NEA description of the commission was somewhat exaggerated. Although the commission did spend some funds during its more than 20 years of existence, at first it handled relatively few cases, preferring mainly to issue statements, usually as a follow-up to investigations made by its 15 members and 44 advisers. Through statements it campaigned for increased teacher salaries; it damned child labor and the teacher shortage; it demanded the establishment of an international office of education. In 1943, however, the commission began work that was to point the way to a vast program of legal support for teacher rights. In that year the commission defended three Oklahoma teachers who were, it said, discharged unfairly. The three, later reinstated, included Kate Frank. As result of the need for legal defense funds that arose from the Oklahoma case, the commission established the Kate Frank

Fund as a source of dollars for teachers in need of legal assistance. Through the late 1940s and the 1950s the commission defended a dozen or so teachers. The Kate Frank Fund soon proved insufficient, and in 1949 NEA began allocating regular monies to the fund, now renamed the DuShane Fund in honor of the 1941 NEA president.

Throughout the 1960s the number of cases handled by NEA and its DuShane Fund increased. By 1968 the number of teacher cases funded by NEA had grown to 68 in one year. In 1969 the number leaped to 130 cases. During 1970 at least 200 teachers whose contracts were terminated without sufficient cause were defended before school boards and in the courts by the DuShane Fund and its lawyers. In addition, AFT's defense fund, though smaller than NEA's, was backing defense efforts for dozens of teachers in the 1960s and 1970s.

The nature of the cases supported by teacher funds ranged over nearly every aspect of personal and professional teacher rights. For example, the teacher's right to free choice of personal appearance was the crux of three cases in 1970. A nontenured Monson, Massachusetts, teacher dismissed from his job for wearing a beard won his case in a decision given by the U.S. District Court for the District of Massachusetts. The decision awarded back pay, compensatory damages, and reinstatement for David Lucia, an eighth grade English teacher. Further, the court ordered the five members of the school committee and the superintendent to pay as individuals more than $2,500 for damages, back pay, and legal costs.

The Massachusetts case set a precedent that prevented a bearded Delaware teacher's case from even going to court. The teacher, backed by his associations, was retained in his job as assistant athletic director in the Seaford, Delaware, schools. On November 17, 1970, the Seaford school board had told Gary White that he must appear clean-shaven to retain his position. Delaware State Education Association officials, appearing before the school board on November 24 with advice from the

NEA Office of General Counsel, defended White's constitutional right to wear his hair as he wished. On December 8 the board announced its change of heart.

An Oklahoma high school social studies teacher who was reprimanded for wearing her skirts too short took her fight regarding nonrenewal of her contract to court with the backing of NEA's DuShane Emergency Fund. Marilyn Tourtellotte claimed that none of her hemlines in question was more than two inches above the knee, the standard set for student dress at Vinita High School. There were no published or announced regulations regarding teacher attire. A jurisdictional brief filed in the U.S. District Court addressed itself to two major questions: Whether a teacher has a constitutional right to dress in any reasonable manner not repugnant to his or her status or employment or inconsistent with classroom decorum, and whether a teacher as a public employee is constitutionally shielded from arbitrary, capricious, and unreasonable governmental action. The brief stated Mrs. Tourtellotte's opinion that the matter of her attire was a constitutionally protected right so long as it was not disruptive of the educational process, that the right to dress within the restrictions of decency was protected by the explicit guarantee of freedom of expression and by the tone and intent of the Bill of Rights, and that procedural due process in this case would require at least a hearing to determine the truth of the charges. The court agreed.

NEA funds also backed teachers who claimed they were treated unjustly because of materials they used in the classroom. In one case, a suit was filed in U.S. District Court on behalf of Ralph Bates, Jr., a nontenured high school English teacher who was fired for using "controversial" materials for class readings or discussions. The challenged materials included Ernest Hemingway's *For Whom the Bell Tolls*, Edward Albee's *The Zoo Story*, and the film-novel *Midnight Cowboy*. The complaint in the Bates case also asserted that he did not receive notification of his employment status or a hearing before the

Silverton [Texas] Independent School District's request for his resignation and its refusal to allow him to teach in that district when he refused to be coerced into resigning. Bates was asked to resign and informed at a later meeting that he had "caused a disturbance in the community and couldn't get along with the administration." The complaint alleged that his constitutional rights of academic freedom and due process had been violated. The district had not announced standards governing proper and improper speech and activity by teachers in the classroom.

In another case, the Michigan State Tenure Commission cleared the record of Wanda Lee Mullins, former head of the English department of Vandercook Lake. She had been charged and found guilty by the Vandercook board of education of "condoning the use of obscenity" in her students' journals and essays. Miss Mullins' teaching approach was designed to reach students who were in danger of becoming dropouts and delinquents. Her attorney argued that Miss Mullins' innovative techniques were at stake, saying, "We must listen to our children and hear what they are saying, not expel students and fire teachers." The commission reversed the decision of the board to remove her from the department chairmanship and suspend her for six months.

The DuShane Fund provided support, too, for teachers mistreated as the result of their activities outside school. For example, the fund provided financial aid to a Florida college professor who was fired after organizing an off-campus antiwar demonstration in the spring of 1973. NEA's fund paid legal fees for Robert Stevenson, a professor in the American Ideas department of the University of South Florida. In a federal court suit filed in Tampa, Stevenson charged that the college administration denied him due process of law and attempted to restrict his freedom of speech. "The basis for decision on this campus runs the rather dubious gamut from whimsey to tyranny," he said. "What we need here is a rule of law to be followed by all, including the president." The suit, which eventually lost in the courts, sought for Stevenson $150,000 in punitive damages, continuation of his teaching contract, and a pledge from the defendants that employees of the university system may express unpopular views "without fear of reprisals." The suit also asked that the defendants be enjoined from denying employees of the university system the rights of due process of law guaranteed under the Fourteenth Amendment.

The NEA fund also provided assistance for three white teachers who were fired after participating in civil rights activities in two all-black Mobile, Alabama, high schools. The DuShane Fund paid legal fees for Donald B. Dickerson, Roy Hyde, and Fred Pistorious, all fired after criticizing the Mobile County school board for mass suspension of black students. In a federal court suit, the three teachers charged that by firing them, board members intended to "curtail and restrict" academic freedom, "chill and depress" freedom of speech, and indicate "what will happen to those under their supervision and control who do not adhere to the board's line in the expression of their views." The suit sought and won for each of the three teachers compensatory and punitive damages, back pay, legal expenses, and new contracts to teach in Mobile County.

NEA expanded its support of teachers into the field of higher education during the 1970s, standing behind college faculty in dozens of cases each year. In a 1970 case, for instance, a former faculty member at Northern Virginia Community College, William P. Haubner, won a $20,000 settlement from the two-year college located in Fairfax County. Haubner, former assistant professor of political science, had charged in a complaint that college officials refused to reappoint him because of his activities in organizing an affiliate of the National Faculty Association of Community and Junior Colleges, an NEA unit. NEA President George D. Fischer hailed the court victory as a "landmark in NEA's battle for teacher rights and academic freedom."

Some 115 separate lawsuits involving college faculty experiencing employment difficulties had received substantial support from the DuShane Fund by 1974. Faculty in community, junior, and four-year colleges and universities were provided with legal assistance, including payment of legal expenses and subsistence loans, to enable them to challenge in the courts adverse administrative actions. Several precedential decisions came out of these suits, the most important the Roth/Sindermann case, which the U.S. Supreme Court decided favorably for faculty members in June, 1972. The court affirmed that faculty members, both tenured and nontenured, might not be denied a new contract because they exercised a constitutional right. The court declared that all faculty dismissed in mid-contract were entitled to reasons and to a hearing. The court also indicated that nontenured faculty members must receive procedural due process before nonrenewal decision involving charges that might seriously damage a faculty member's standing and associations in the community or impose a stigma harming future job opportunities. The court further held that if the employer's practices or policies created a *de facto* tenure situation, reasons and a hearing were mandatory. Sindermann settled his suit against Odessa Junior College in Texas for $48,000 in back pay and attorney's fees.

NEA also pursued litigation in 1974 to ensure that all teachers were accorded the fair treatment required by the Roth/Sindermann decisions and to further clarify the procedural rights of faculty. Among the cases it supported was one calling for back pay and reinstatement for Minnesota junior college instructor Gary Wellner. And Philip Ortwein won a permanent injunction in federal court requiring the president of the University of South Florida to provide him a full due process hearing before discharge. The court found that the reasons supplied for denial of tenure more than three years earlier constituted a denial of his liberty to pursue his career. Massive staff cuts, allegedly for budgetary and performance reasons, at the University of Wisconsin at Oshkosh were under legal investigation, with funds supplied by NEA and its Wisconsin affiliates. Reductions in force at Miami-Dade Community College were challenged in the Fifth Circuit. Four nonrenewed faculty members alleged that nonrenewal decisions were based on subjective factors. Several faculty association organizers also charged administrative harassment. Within the higher education area, the DuShane Fund also channeled its resources against antinepotism rules, salary inequities, and discriminatory maternity leave policies. Antinepotism practices were under attack because they discriminated against women by forcing colleges to choose between spouses, with the husband invariably obtaining tenure or a promotion and the wife relinquishing her career. In one such case, a former instructor, Aino Jarvesoo, lost her position because her husband was already a tenured member of the faculty at the University of Massachusetts at Amherst. She was reinstated with full benefits.

Arbitrary firings and nonrenewals that follow exercise of First Amendment rights were challenged with NEA support. Shirley Schell's allegations that her dismissal from Delaware Technical Community College was in retaliation for joining colleagues in signing a complaint of sex and race discrimination against the college and for criticizing the college administration were upheld by a federal district court. The court, ordering her reinstatement, declared that the termination had "no factual support and not only was for a reason unrelated to her employment, but also was for federal protected activity." Patrick Dougherty, in another free speech case, received a back pay settlement from the University of Missouri at Columbia. A political science instructor, he was dismissed in mid-contract for his activities protesting participation of the university's band and football team in a parade sponsored by an allegedly racist organization. In another case, NEA and the Maryland State Teachers Association assisted Roger M. Shaw and Richard A. Winn, former Frederick Community College professors, in their lawsuit seeking reinstatement and lost salary. They charged that their dismissals were in reprisal for exercise of their First Amendment rights. During the spring of 1973 Shaw and Winn urged faculty senate members to protest the college trustees' refusal to grant negotiation rights to the faculty. As a result, 32 faculty members attended commencement exercises without academic regalia. Subsequently the college attempted to fire all of them. Shaw and Winn actually were fired, but they won their case.

Illegal spending of faculty retirement funds, including crediting interest on the teachers' money to the employers' account, was challenged successfully in a suit filed by the Los Angeles College Teachers Association against the Los Angeles Community College District. The DuShane Fund and the California Teachers Association provided financial aid in this legal battle in state court to recover funds for the 2,500-member faculty. The board was further charged with not fully informing certified employees about the consequences of joining the state retirement system.

Desegregation Cases

NEA was also pursuing legal cases supporting desegregation of schools and the displacement of black teachers that often followed desegregation. For example, in 1970 NEA lauded the U.S. Supreme Court's unanimous affirmation that busing might be used as a means of desegregating public schools. The court's decision, which overturned a North Carolina law prohibiting busing of pupils to achieve racial balance, closely followed principles argued in "friend of the court" briefs filed by NEA. NEA backed U.S. District Court Judge James B. McMillan's right to required satellite zoning, crosstown busing, and pairing of schools to integrate the Charlotte school system and urged repeal of the state's antibusing statute. In decisions in the Charlotte-Mecklenburg County (North Carolina), Mobile (Alabama), and Clark County (Georgia) cases, the Supreme Court made its first comprehensive review of school desegregation since the historic 1954 ruling. The new ruling gave federal judges broad powers to order a variety of means to end legally established school segregation when school authorities failed to eliminate one-race schools or to show that their existence did not result from past discriminatory action. The court also said that racial ratios might be used as a starting point in establishing an acceptable desegregation plan. And the court ordered school officials to foster integration by different measures, such as gerrymandering school attendance lines and establishing noncontiguous school zones.

NEA involvement here, on behalf of the principles of desegregation, was just one example of its concern in this area. From 1966 to 1973 NEA, through its teacher rights division, supported the rights of black educators who experienced employment difficulties ranging from outright dismissal to demotions and reassignment. NEA worked with NAACP and other civic rights groups in desegregation and faculty rights efforts. Of approximately $2.6 million allocated by the DuShane Fund from 1970 to 1973, nearly three-quarters of a million dollars was spent to assist displaced educators and to facilitate the desegregation process. In addition, investigations were conducted in areas where massive displacement of black educators had taken place. Legal redress was secured, for example, for black educators in South Carolina and Mississippi who failed to achieve arbitrary cut-off scores on the National Teachers Examination and the Graduate Record Examination. Other court rulings required school districts to rehire dismissed teachers with back pay and to actively recruit black faculty to achieve equitable ratios of white-to-black staff. NEA intervened as party plaintiff in school desegregation suits in Alabama and filed motions in courts to protect the rights of black educators.

Meanwhile, in 1970 the U.S. Supreme Court, concurring with NEA briefs, affirmed a lower court's decision that New York state's antibusing law was unconstitutional. The statute barred appointed school boards and state authorities from using busing to achieve racial balance in the state's public schools. NEA, the Buffalo Teachers Federation, and the New York State Teachers Association in "friends of the court" briefs supported a suit initiated by the NAACP and five parents against Buffalo and New York state education officials. The federal court judges held that the statute "constitutes an explicit and invidious racial classification and denies equal protection of the law." The court's order was its first action on segregation arising from housing patterns (*de facto* segregation).

NEA also monitored school desegregation when asked by its affiliates. During the 1970–71 school year, the Mississippi Teachers Association and the Louisiana Education Association asked NEA to set up a task force to check on court-ordered desegregation in the two states. The 21-member task force traveled throughout the area and reported in November that, as schools in Mississippi and Louisiana desegregated, black authority within the schools disintegrated. As a consequence, school desegregation in Louisiana and Mississippi has produced the "near total disintegration of black authority in every area . . . of public education." The task force's report, a 43-page document, charged that the bad news about desegregation in the two states "tragically outweighs the good." In the south the early stages of a unitary school system "are affecting the education of black youth, the professional expectations of the black educators, and the economic and political aspirations of Southern black communities in a way that could not have been anticipated during the long struggle for integrated education." According to the report, black authority has melted in the face of "zealously guarded white control over economic resources, political resources, and public serving institutions." The task force found that in neither Louisiana nor Mississippi were racial discrimination tactics "subtle enough to hide the malignancy of its continued existence as school systems move into their first and second years of desegregation."

Other actions for civil and human rights included protection of individual educators who experienced discrimination. Dozens of such cases were pursued; a suit won on behalf of nine Starkville, Mississippi, teachers provides an example. NEA, the

Mississippi Teachers Association, and the teachers won a landmark ruling in federal court when the judge held unconstitutional a Starkville school board policy requiring employed teachers and applicants for teaching positions to have either minimum scores on the Graduate Record Examination or a master's degree in order to be retained or hired. The court struck down the board's policy, holding that use of the test violated the equal protection and due process clauses of the Fourteenth Amendment. The nine black Starkville teachers who were not rehired in 1970 after failing to make minimum cutoff scores set by the school board on the Graduate Record Examination were ordered reinstated to their former positions for the remainder of the year and for 1971–72. After hearing testimony, the judge issued a preliminary injunction ordering the school board to reinstate the teachers who had not found jobs in other school districts. The court held that because the Graduate Record Examination was not designed as a means to select elementary and secondary teachers, measure preparation for teaching, or identify professional competency or effectiveness, the school board's policy imposed "arbitrary and unreasonable qualifications" for employment of faculty.

PREGNANT TEACHERS' RIGHTS

One final example of legal defense actions on behalf of teacher rights underlines organized teachers' concern for women's rights—a concern important to a profession whose members, even in the 1970s, were more than 60 percent female. In February, 1974, the U.S. Supreme Court struck down mandatory maternity leave provisions for leaves of absence, regardless of an individual's ability to continue work, as violations of the Fourteenth Amendment's guarantee of due process of law. NEA President Helen Wise hailed the decision in favor of three teachers as "the greatest advance for female teachers since married teachers gained the right to teach." NEA had invested more than $25,000 in district, appellate, and

Supreme Court legal battles in the cases that culminated in the decision; AFT joined in the amicus brief in the Supreme Court. NEA initiated and fully financed the Susan Cohen case (Chesterfield County, Virginia) from its beginning in 1971 and shared with Women's Law Fund the legal expenses in the case of Ohioans Jo Carol La Fleur and Elizabeth Nelson. "The ruling means," said NEA President Wise, "that pregnant teachers who can work and want to work will no longer be compelled to leave their jobs a specified number of months before the scheduled birth. The educational process will be enhanced by this ruling, since teachers free from unreasonable restrictions are better able to provide the type of instruction that parents, teacher, and students want. This ruling encourages NEA to continue its efforts to attack sex discrimination in other areas, such as sex role stereotyping in textbooks, failure to promote women teachers with qualifications equal to men, and antinepotism practices that cause the female spouse to lose her job."

The Supreme Court concluded in the case that the two arguments school boards provided for mandatory leave policies —firm cut-off dates were necessary to maintain continuity of classroom instruction and some teachers became physically incapable of adequately performing certain of their duties during the latter part of pregnancy—could not justify sweeping mandatory leave regulations which "employ irrefutable presumptions that unduly penalize a female for deciding to bear a child." The Court noted that many pregnant teachers were capable of working, that administrative reasons alone were inadequate to deny a woman her rights, and that the arbitrary cut-off dates "have no rational relationship to the valid state interest of preserving continuity of instruction. As long as the teacher is required to give substantial advance notice of her condition," the Court continued, "the choice of firm dates later in pregnancy would serve the board's objectives just as well, while imposing a far lesser burden on the women's exercise of constitutionally protected freedom."

As a result of the maternity cases, by 1975 courts in several states had ruled that school districts that had required women to leave teaching against their will during pregnancy must pay the teachers for the time they would have been in the classroom had they not been forced to resign. In Oklahoma City alone, NEA officials estimated, back pay for dozens of women teachers could run to a million dollars.

13 / The Causes of

Teacher Militancy

W<small>HAT HAS CAUSED TEACHER MILITANCY?</small>

From the beginning, American teacher groups have been schizophrenic, dividing their concerns between improving education in general and fighting for more pay and benefits. Yet, despite this divided focus between principles and pocketbooks, teacher activism through the years has reflected to a great extent the more practical motive of economic gain. From the first NEA salary study at the beginning of the twentieth century to the detailed annual reports prepared by NEA research in the 1970s, documents comparing and contrasting teachers' salaries have been best sellers throughout the profession. The relationship between economic stress on teachers and increasing militancy showed itself in the rash of strikes after each World War. In these periods of inflation (and after World War I, inflation followed by depression), teachers became more active; they formed unions, they joined associations in large numbers —in short, they reacted as other citizens do when their pocketbooks are threatened.

Few who have examined or commented upon teacher

militancy have ignored the dollar as a cause. NEA staff leader
T. M. Stinnett, whose ties with teachers' causes span several
generations, cited money as the number one reason for their
militancy:

> The mounting impatience of teachers with what they consider to
> be economic injustice is a factor of considerable significance. The
> point of view here is that teacher salaries have historically lagged
> behind the returns to other comparable groups, and often behind
> the pay of unskilled workers. Teachers dislike the resistance of the
> public to reasonable adjustments in their pay in an affluent society
> which they have had a significant part in creating. As a quite
> general practice, soothing phrases about the importance of teachers
> has been proffered them in lieu of increased economic rewards. It is
> obvious that teachers have increasingly taken the position that they
> will no longer rely solely upon boards and legislatures for adequate
> remuneration, but will themselves become vigorously involved in
> the search for economic justice.

NEA President Braulio Alonso agreed with this analysis.
"We live in the most affluent society this nation has ever
known, and the teacher is not an active participant in the
affluency," he said in 1968. "The average teachers' salary in the
United States is $7,295. Yet the U.S. Bureau of Labor recently
stated that a family of four needed about $9,200 a year to live
moderately. How many teachers do we know who make
$9,200?" Paul Woodring, then education editor of the *Satur-
day Review*, summarized the causes of teacher discontent this
way: "What do the teachers want? The obvious answer to the
last question is 'more money.'"

George Counts, analyzing teacher strikes in 1947, named
the deteriorating relative economic position of teachers as the
number one reason for teacher activism. *Look* magazine senior
editor Jack Star, who surveyed the nation to examine "Our
Angry Teachers" in 1968, concluded, "Although there are many
reasons for teacher dissatisfaction, low salaries are primarily
responsible for teacher militancy." Writer Jim Hampton made
a similar survey in 1968 for *The National Observer*. His

conclusion: "Dissatisfaction with salaries is a constant factor in most teachers' walkouts." One of the most detailed studies of teacher strikes, Albert Schiff's "A Study and Evaluation of Teachers' Strikes in the United States," concluded, "The basic immediate causes of teachers' strikes were economic." A less detailed study by William Moore and Ray Marshall in 1973 also identified salary lags as a major reason for growth of the American Federation of Teachers.

Among observers who have cited lack of money as a cause of teacher militancy, however, few have been willing to say that money alone was the cause. Stinnett, for example, though he placed economic injustice first on his list of reasons for militancy, included in his list five other reasons. NEA President Alonso added four reasons, though he too placed economic injustice number one. *Saturday Review* editor-at-large Woodring added these words: "But money is not the complete answer. Behind the strikes are more subtle causes of long standing which have contributed notably to the lowering of teacher morale." The 1947 analysis by George Counts included seven noneconomic reasons for teacher strikes. Schiff's study, though identifying salary as the basic and immediate cause of teacher strikes, added, "Teachers' strikes have a multiplicity of causes." Elizabeth D. Koontz, while NEA president-elect in 1968, denied that salary was the number one cause behind teacher militancy. Speaking on the "Today" show, she said, "Well, you know, surprisingly enough, there are people in this country who still do not realize that teachers did not place salary as number one. Now don't misunderstand me—salary is in there—right at the top. But first of all, conditions of work and financial support of schools. And this means that counties are unable to use property tax as a base for the educational system. And so they are asking the state to make a bigger financial floor. And this is almost in every case."

Ronald G. Corwin, an Ohio State sociologist, has studied extensively the implications of teacher militancy in the United

States. He suggested in 1969 one reason salary alone did not motivate the militant teacher.

Incongruence among statuses has become a critical feature of our society. Where there is no longer a close connection between various dimensions of status such as salary, authority, and level of education, winning salary increments, for example, does not in itself provide access to power. It can be assumed, then, that a group compares its achievements in one area not only with the achievements of other people, but also with its achievements in other areas. Hence, teachers are likely to consider their standing in education relative to their salary, occupational prestige, and authority. Increases which teachers may have made in their authority do not seem to have kept pace with their advances in salary and education in recent years. Such a discrepancy could be an important incentive behind their recent efforts to achieve new levels of authority . . . from a strictly bargaining point of view, one might have expected that the recent salary increments compensate teachers for their low authority and prestige; however, we have seen that within the congruence framework, a salary increase may simply encourage employees to achieve other forms of advancement.

PROFESSIONALISM

Thus salary increases are not the single motivating force behind teacher militancy; but the achievement of a salary gain leads only to more militancy—added efforts to reach other goals. Corwin's thesis assumes that teachers have become more professional in order to be recognized. "Professionalization," he says, "represents one very effective means by which members of an occupation can utilize their special knowledge as a lever for improving the relative position of their occupation." This growing professionalism of teachers as a cause of militancy was noted some years ago. Counts, in his 1947 analysis, said, "A vast range of professional and semiprofessional occupations more highly rewarded than teaching has appeared." He mentioned engineering, clerical trades, and technical occupations. Further, Counts said, "Teaching is no longer a stepping-stone job—the

194

average number of years in service has risen from four or five to ten or fifteen." In addition the level of preparation for teaching, which affects the number of years necessary for preparation, has increased since Counts made his comments.

In 1947 when Counts was writing, only 44.3 percent of American public school teachers had earned a bachelor's degree and only 15.1 percent had advanced degrees. By the 1955–56 school year these percentages had increased to 53.2 holding bachelor's degrees and 24.6 holding master's and doctor's degrees. By 1965 more than 90 percent of all U.S. public school teachers had at least a four-year bachelor's degree.

Another factor contributing to the growing professionalism of teachers was the increase in the percentage of teachers who were males. Male teachers had accounted for only 17 percent of all classroom teachers in the middle 1920s, but by 1965 they had increased to more than 30 percent. More dramatically, the growth in number of male teachers from 1954 to 1964 was 93 percent, compared to 38 percent for females during the same period. A study by Alan Rosenthal indicated, "Male teachers are more likely to join a union than are females." He explained that there could be many reasons why this was so and why schools with a large proportion of men faculty facilitated union membership. Among the most important, he said, is that men have greater need of the benefits, particularly monetary ones, which unions offered public school teachers. And because they are more likely than women to carry weighty financial burdens, men apparently have the greater incentive to join militant organizations and a greater willingness to fight for immediate monetary gains. Rosenthal also suggested that younger teachers were more militant than older ones. Because the median age of American teachers fell in the post-World War II years, this could be an added factor in militancy.

BUREAUCRATIZATION

Rising teacher militancy was also spurred by the growth in size and bureaucratization of the schools. The new professional teacher, determined to improve teaching and learning, found that growing urbanization, consolidation of schools, and sheer size of the educational enterprise blocked efforts. With the growth of the educational enterprise came a tendency to impose bureaucratic regulation.

At this point the development of the educational system reflected contradictory pressures. On one hand, increased size and responsibility led the educational organization to formalize its operation by specifying exactly how employees should behave in coordinating their contributions to it. On the other hand, the organization attracted highly trained professionals who needed and expected authority and freedom to make their own decisions in solving uniquely varying problems. Because highly detailed prescriptions restricted the ability to work effectively, the professional resisted the emphasis on control and regulation which is part of a bureaucracy. Professionals began to demand the right to participate in decisions that determined their status and destiny in the organization. And they were not without power to back up their point of view, since the organization now depended on the availability of their specialized skills.

Increasing size and bureaucratization of the schools also meant that school administration became more difficult. At the same time, the increasing democratization of administrative practices was straining the leadership abilities of administrators. Thus collective negotiation by teachers is partly an answer to the increasingly difficult job of the school administrator to communicate; in effect, negotiations become the channel of communication between the administrator and the staff. NEA's Stinnett made this point strongly, saying that collective negotiations by teachers "constitute another evolutionary step in the democratizing of school administration." AFT leaders have used similar arguments to urge unionization of school staffs. The professional teacher is organizing "to lengthen his shadow" and "to combat the dehumanizing effects" of being the employee of a large, impersonal organization, one union leader said in 1967. Another said that the value of a union was that teachers, by united action with others, became partners in an enterprise that promoted the general welfare of all citizens. Thus, the union teacher was no longer an isolated unit in the vast bureaucracy that educational systems have become.

OTHER CAUSES

From organizational beginnings, through the efforts by state associations in the early part of the twentieth century to win tenure rights, minimum salary schedules, and continuing contract laws by establishing mandatory negotiation, teachers have been able to move only as fast as their unions and associations. And, during the past 35 years, these groups have changed greatly. In 1941 the NEA National Commission for the Defense of Teacher Rights was founded. In 1946 the first teacher strike for bargaining rights took place in Connecticut. In 1961 the United Federation of Teachers won control over New York City teachers, an event followed by the establishment of an NEA urban group the same year. In 1962 President John F. Kennedy signed Executive Order 10988, permitting federal government officials to unionize and encouraging the growth of white-collar unions in government. The same year sanctions were approved as official NEA policy.

These changes led to changes in the posture taken by teachers. As their unions and associations became more militant and better equipped to fight for teachers, the teachers themselves responded with added militancy. Starting in 1961, the two major national teacher groups, the AFT and the NEA, began a struggle to win the minds and moneys of teachers. Each tried to outtalk and outmaneuver the other, meanwhile claiming to be more militant. Some have labeled this competition itself as a major cause of teacher militancy. *Saturday Review* editor James Cass, writing with Max Birnbaum, director of Boston University's Human Relations Laboratory, said in 1968, "To date, the growing militancy of teachers has been explained primarily in terms of the mounting competition for members and power between the small but rapidly growing American Federation of Teachers, an AFL-CIO affiliate, and the larger, professionally oriented National Education Association." Stanley Elam, editor of the *Phi Delta Kappan*, said in 1964 that no one could say with certainty whether the NEA or the AFT would emerge the eventual winner in the accelerating rivalry. One thing seemed certain, though, he said: Teachers are breaking the master-servant pattern that once characterized their relationship with boards of education.

Any examination of causes of teacher activism must also consider the availability of mechanisms—the tools available to teachers. Desire without method is sterile. Militant teachers—younger, more of them male, more professional, better organized, economically deprived—could act only when the mechanisms for that action were available. State laws requiring school boards to bargain with teachers became, from 1955, the major mechanism for translating militant desire into militant action. By November, 1964, approximately 100,000 teachers were working under contracts negotiated with school boards. By the beginning of the 1968–69 school year more than 925,000 teachers in 43 percent of the nation's school districts enrolling 1,000 pupils or more were covered by such contracts. By 1973 more than 1.5 million teachers had negotiated contracts. In 1970 the use of strikes by teachers as a means of enforcing their negotiation rights was fully defended both by union and association spokesmen.

The Social Climate

In addition to these causes—economic injustice, increasing professionalism, growth in size and bureaucratization in schools, changes in teacher organizations, and the availability of mechanisms—there was one other influence on teacher militancy in the post-World War II years. This was the social setting, the framework in which teacher militancy operated in American society.

Important to this setting was how teachers viewed themselves. The nineteenth century American teacher existed in a genteel tradition that led society to expect him to be quiet, moral, apolitical, and penniless. In the period from the death of Lincoln until World War I, the educational philosophy of America's schools largely fit the needs of the status quo. In the 1920s and 1930s the influence of the Depression and the consequent loss of business support for the schools, combined with the progressive education movement, led the schools to a more activist position. By 1947 teachers felt a deep resentment toward the community and believed they were not appreciated. In 1968 John Gardner said, "It has been fashionable to blame educators for every shortcoming of the schools, but educators cannot maintain standards of excellence in a community that cares more about a marching band and a winning basketball team than it does about teachers' salaries."

Teachers also were responding to what they thought was the public's unrealistic demand that educators should be solving all the growing problems of a complex society. M. Chester Nolte, writing for the *School Board Journal* in 1965, described this pressure on teachers:

Our commitment of education is sizeable, but there are many educational problems—overcrowded classrooms, double sessions, underpaid teachers, rundown facilities, inadequate financing, and similar failings. Teachers cannot fail to see a discrepancy between our avowed faith in education and the sorry state into which some of our public schools have fallen. Pressures have been exerted on teachers to solve some of these problems, but many are problems over which teachers in all fairness have little if any control. The civil rights and separation of state issues are noteworthy examples of this type of problem. The effect has been an implied disappointment with, if not condemnation of, the teaching staff at a time when some comparatively serious problems are facing public education.

By 1967 observers were noting a progressive alienation of teachers from the school and the community. Middle-class, status quo values no longer satisfied the teacher. James Cass, then education editor of the *Saturday Review*, mentioned an aspect of this changing social setting, a factor he called "the changing etiquette of social protest." What he meant by this, he told editors at an Educational Press Association meeting, was the acceptance by teachers and by society at large of the protest actions taken by civil rights workers. Notre Dame alumnus Robert W. Neirnyck, writing to fellow lawyers in the *Notre Dame Lawyer*, made this point well: "A more general reason for the upswing in teacher strikes," he said, "is the increased use of militancy by minority groups throughout the nation. This is most notable in the civil rights and anti-Vietnam protestations. . . . These massed displays of power have not gone unnoticed by teachers who . . . see other power blocs getting their share not through reasonableness but by belligerence."

Add to these conditions two other specific changes in the social setting itself: a growing general approval by the public of teachers' right to strike and the existence of a mobile, more cosmopolitan populace. In these ways, a changed social setting has meant, in NEA President Braulio Alonso's words, "today's teacher is convinced he can change the destiny of his profession only by taking an active part in determining what happens to him and to education."

MULTIPLE CAUSES

The causes of teacher militancy in the United States, then, are multiple. Five of these basic causes are: 1) economic injustice to teachers for a long period of time; 2) growing professionalism of teachers as their role assumed a larger meaning in an increasingly complex society; 3) corresponding growth in the size of schools and of the bureaucratization within the schools; 4) changes within teachers' groups and especially the democratization that led to a stronger role within them for the classroom teachers; 5) and the availability of mechanisms such as negotiation agreements, sanctions, and legal counsel increasingly enabling teachers to fight for their goals. These five causes grew not separately but together; they brought about change not óne by one, but jointly. Alone, none of the five might have brought about the extent of teacher militancy seen in the 1960s and 1970s; together, their interrelated strength was great.

The five causes fed upon one another; each affected the others and vice versa. The growing professionalism of teachers, for example, fed teachers' desires for more adequate salaries; the struggle for more adequate salaries led to the establishment of mechanisms to ensure economic gains. Similarly, the need for such mechanisms brought about changes in teacher groups as they expanded to provide the services necessary for these mechanisms. And the expansion of the teacher groups, combined with the increase in the mechanisms, led to increasing educational bureaucracy as school administrations explored new roles to meet the requirements of teacher negotiations, grievance procedures, and the like.

The same reciprocal relationship can be seen from another angle. The growing professionalism of teachers led to demands for new types of teacher services and new teacher roles, which in turn led to further bureaucratization of the schools. This growing bureaucratization helped encourage the growth of teacher groups as the teacher reached out for organizational help in attempts to deal with a faceless bureaucracy. This growth allowed unions and associations to develop the mechanisms such as negotiation agreements and bargaining laws that would help give teachers a say in determining their economic future, thus raising teachers' salaries. Finally, better salaries raised the teacher's own image of himself and of his role as a professional.

Similar examples of the interrelatedness of the causes can be drawn from almost any pair of them. For instance, many of the mechanisms developed by teachers directly affected their professional role. To cite just one example, many negotiation agreements included requirements relating to the instructional role of the teacher, requirements designed to enhance the professional role of the teacher. Conversely, it was the desire of the teachers to enhance their professional role that led to the inclusion of such requirements in negotiation agreements.

Added to these five interrelated causes of teacher militancy is one more element to give the whole story of teacher militancy's growth—the social setting in which the causes were acting. By the 1960s the social climate was ripe for action by teachers. The nation's economy was strong and could support demands for higher salaries. Many state laws now allowed public employees the right to negotiate, if not to strike. President Kennedy gave federal public employees the right to organize and negotiate. And the public image of the teacher was high: He was seen, for instance, as a weapon in the Cold War, a trainer of minds to build scientists. In this setting, teacher militancy, brought to an action stage by the causes outlined here, moved into a new phase—into a time when teacher unions and associations could call strikes that tied up entire cities and states, when teachers' lawyers could demand rights and carry those demands to the Supreme Court, when organized teachers could at last make many of the decisions that affected their classroom and out-of-classroom lives. It was a long way from genteel poverty to first-class citizenship, and organized power had been the key to it.

14 / The Future of

Teacher Power

WHAT OF THE FUTURE OF TEACHER MILITANCY?

The mechanism of teacher militancy has been organization. That mechanism will continue to grow. By 1975, approximately two million American public school teachers were members of AFT or NEA or both. In that year, NEA completed its unification of affiliates, which meant that every teacher who joined a local or state education association also joined NEA. NEA membership stood at nearly 1.7 million in 1975; it will rise to 1.8 million or more within the decade. AFT membership in 1975 was approximately 450,000, though more than 200,000 of these were also NEA members in the "merged" state of New York.

In addition to public school teachers, kindergarten through twelfth grade, there are 230,000 nonpublic teachers and 600,000 college teachers in the nation. Organizers have paid little attention to the nonpublic teachers, but both NEA and AFT have begun to nibble at the college faculty, especially in the public colleges and the junior and community colleges. As of 1975, however, most college faculty remained unorganized—some standing intellectually above the fray, some believers in an independent faculty senate, some members of the American Association of University Professors, a group that only in the mid-1970s began to accept the idea of collective bargaining. This will change, and by 1980 most college faculty will be organized by NEA, AFT, AAUP, or a combination of these groups.

The major unanswered question about college faculty organizing in 1975 was whether AAUP would merge its higher education efforts with those of AFT or NEA. Both teacher groups had been wooing AAUP; a decision was likely in a year or two. Once that matter was settled, college organizing would move faster, for faculty members desiring to remain unorganized would have nowhere to turn; they would be faced with deciding only which group would bargain for them.

Thus, by 1983, nearly all public school teachers—2.345 million of them, according to the National Center for Education Statistics—will be members of a national union, either NEA or AFT. At least half of the 637,000 college faculty members in 1983 will have joined their elementary and secondary school peers as union members. Only the relatively small number—234,000—of private school teachers will remain unorganized.

COLLECTIVE BARGAINING

More important, these two-and-a-half million educators will be engaged in collective bargaining.

By the 1968-69 school year, more than a million teachers and other educators were employed in public school systems having teacher-school board negotiation agreements; by the 1972-73 school year, this number was nearly one-and-a-half million. By 1970 statewide negotiation laws were on the books in state after state, including Alaska, California, Connecticut, Florida, Maryland, Massachusetts, Michigan, Minnesota, Nebraska, New Hampshire, New Jersey, New York, Oregon,

Rhode Island, Texas, Washington, and Wisconsin. By 1974, NEA was pressing for a federal statute to require negotiation with teacher groups, and AFT was urging use of federal labor statutes for teacher bargaining. Public officials were recognizing the public employee's right to bargain with the government. "That people have the right to organize seems to me an incontestable fact in 1975," Secretary of Labor John Dunlop told teachers.

It is uncontestable, too, that this trend will continue. Arrangements for teacher bargaining do exist, have existed, and will continue to exist and increase in various forms. A University of California, Los Angeles, labor relations analyst, Donald L. Martin, made this inference in 1967 based on his consideration of the sellers'-conclusion model, which is used to study political behavior of unions. Martin surveyed the origins and growth of collective teacher activity, applied the sellers'-conclusion model to the directions of that activity, and reported that the model suggested nothing to contradict the expectation of greater teacher militancy in the future. He said: "Two points seem clear. The union movement in education has had a rebirth, encouraged by a wave of success; and school administrators and boards of education are experiencing a new competitive force in determining educational policy."

Newly organized college and university professors will find themselves rubbing elbows with public school teachers in the rush toward collective bargaining. Participants at a 1974 New York City conference sponsored by the National Center for the Study of Collective Bargaining in Higher Education were just one group who saw college bargaining as part of the new direction, involving "substantial changes in the professor's image of self and career."

Critics of teacher collective bargaining have accused them of wanting exactly what all unions want: more. And it is true that teacher unions continue to ask for more money and more power. But this is only part of the story. True, teacher bargainers will continue to focus on higher salaries and better fringe benefits. A study of salaries earned in one year by Michigan teachers, for example, showed that collective bargaining had paid substantial dividends—up to 20 percent. The same study saw these salary gains as only the beginning, since they were won without general increases in state support of the schools. Teachers in the future will turn to state legislatures and to a broader state tax base for increases in salaries. So there is no sign of a reversal of this trend toward bargaining gains on the economic front.

But the spectrum of teacher bargaining has become very broad. By the early 1970s, teacher unions were negotiating contracts that included, in addition to salary and fringe benefits, other items ranging from safeguards against racial and sexual discrimination to guarantees of consultation and involvement of the teacher group in any plan to change school board policies and regulations. Other guarantees frequently imbedded in the contract were check-off of dues deductions, guarantees for the use of school building and facilities by the union, and teacher time off for grievance procedures or organizational business. Also guaranteed in some contracts were the teacher's right to conduct himself as he sees fit outside the school, the right of political activity and involvement in curriculum review, the employment of specified numbers of educational specialists and/or teacher aides, involvement of teachers in textbook selection, added purchase of instructional aids, secretarial and clerical assistance, guaranteed planning periods, assured time for lunch, development of in-service programs for teachers, seniority guarantees, and sabbatical leaves.

Another aspect of teacher bargaining lies in the answer to the question: Who does the bargaining for teachers? Before 1970, most teachers who were bargaining did their own negotiating; they selected a negotiation committee and it sat down with the team representing the school system. From 1970 on, this method of bargaining was increasingly replaced by bargaining through attorneys and negotiation experts hired by teachers—and matched on the other side of the table by other "hired guns." By 1975, affiliates of NEA had more than 1,000 full-time staff (NEA called them UniServ workers) to call on. Many of these men and women were lawyers; all were trained by NEA to bargain hard and skillfully. AFT staff were similarly trained. Some 2,000 teacher bargainers existed in the nation by the mid-1970s; it was a newly created job, and with a pay scale starting above $15,000, it was attracting high-quality personnel.

The teacher in 1983 will not only be represented by a union; he will also be represented in nearly every case by a trained negotiator.

THE RESULTS OF BARGAINING

Where will all this collective bargaining lead? In the long run, it will lead, among other things, to fewer strikes by teachers, greater professionalism of educators, higher teacher morale, an enlarged role in the school for the teacher, and higher salaries for school personnel.

Fewer strikes and less disruption of schooling are likely because, as a mechanism for handling problems is developed, the chances for peaceful solution of difficulties increases. A *Business Week* columnist pointed out in 1967, applying to the public sector what has happened in the private, that the development of mechanisms to handle employee dissent leads to fewer disruptions. He said: "The labor market operates much the same in the public sector as in the private; perhaps the key to a realistic public approach to public employee unionism lies in that fact. A body of knowledge and law regarding collective bargaining has grown up in the past 35 years. Over the long haul . . . it has contributed to industrial peace and efficiency. Much of this experience should be applicable to the public sector." NEA President James Harris reinforced this point in 1975 when, speaking for a federal collective bargaining law, he said: "Absence of a collective bargaining bill invites frustration, and I think strikes grow out of frustration."

Frederick R. Livingston, a managing partner of a New

207

York City law firm and an attorney with long experience in teacher bargaining, also considers long-term chances for peace in public education good because teacher groups, school boards, and administrators are working to gain the skills required to make negotiation work. He told a seminar in 1968:

> The marked lack of expertise in this area on the part of both public employers and employee organizations has served only to precipitate these head-on confrontations. As New York's Taylor Committee has consistently found, the creation of constructive employee relations in the public sector is ultimately dependent upon the ability of the participants to educate their own members in the art of negotiation and to revise their present programs. . . . I foresee the time when school boards and teachers will reevaluate the educational needs of the children in light of the changing times, when school boards will recognize the need for participation by teachers in this evolutionary, if not revolutionary, process. I foresee the time when there will be general recognition not only by school boards but by the public as a whole of the need for a teaching force of superior caliber with high morale achieved through good salaries, good working conditions, and recognition of the human dignity that is achieved through participation in the educational process.

Also contributing to a lessening of disruptive teacher behavior is the belief, among leaders of teacher groups and American labor at large, that not all disruptions have been effective. Phares E. Reeder, then executive secretary of the West Virginia Education Association, discussing the 1967–68 Florida statewide walkout, said, "Shouts and clamor, picket signs and the no-holds-barred approach may bring temporary victory, but the aftermath can be nasty and long lasting. The Florida fiasco is a good example—and now divisiveness of the worst order prevails." AFL-CIO leader George Meany spoke publicly in 1974 of the lessening value of the strike. And a portent of this move away from the strike could be seen in Hawaii in 1974, when the public employee bargaining law there was modified to require arbitration without job disruption as the final step to bargaining.

Actually, teacher demands for strikes were tempered by the mid-1970s. With other public employees, they were talking not about "striking" but about "the right to strike." And even that was toned down in some cases. When the Coalition of American Public Employees (co-founded by NEA) issued a background paper in 1974 on the need for federal bargaining legislation, it summarized its position on strikes with these less-than-threatening words: "The Coalition—and most other unions—insist on public employees' right to strike. But they agree this right must be tempered by a responsibility to maintain emergency services. The Coalition favors giving a public employees' union the right to choose, at some stage in the bargaining process, binding arbitration as an alternative to exercising the right to strike." Further, one NEA source estimated that 80 percent of the teacher strikes in 1974 were called "just for the right to be heard." Once public bargaining laws get on the books nationwide, the right of a union to be heard would no longer be an issue, and strikes should diminish.

Indeed, by the mid-1970s, it was not the danger of strikes that struck fear into the hearts of some school board members, school administrators, and citizen groups; it was the recognition that teachers wanted something else. They were demanding the full right to bargain as blue-collar workers had been bargaining for years. Thus, at meetings of the National School Boards Association (NSBA), the American Association of School Administrators (AASA), and the National Committee for Citizens in Education, speakers were talking much less about strikes and fulminating more about the horrors of collective bargaining itself. NSBA's delegate assembly in 1975 officially opposed "any and all federal teacher negotiations legislation" and heard delegates argue that children were the hostages during collective bargaining. Commenting on NSBA's meeting and on a Gallup survey taken for NSBA that revealed little public understanding of school boards, AFT President Albert Shanker said, "The NSBA report betrays a paranoia in school board officialdom, the fear that the whole educational system will crumble if the boards lose their absolute power."

School administrators in 1975 seemed only slightly more receptive to teacher bargaining than board members. AASA delegates, though agreeing that teachers have the right to legal defense in the case of dismissal, a voice in policy making, and the right to be accorded respect and dignity, deplored federal collective bargaining legislation. An AASA consultant, Baruch College professor Myron Lieberman, suggested that if teachers got a federal bargaining law their benefits under state statutes should be repealed.

The National Committee for Citizens in Education, meanwhile, was denying the appropriateness of applying private sector negotiation patterns to the public schools and calling for an active voice for the public in teacher bargaining. A conservative teachers' group, the National Association of Professional Educators (NAPE), also expressed this view. "Collective bargaining will take the power of control of the public schools from the citizens and the elected boards of education," said the president of one local NAPE group. "Collective bargaining by teachers will deprive children of precious school time to which they are entitled." (NAPE didn't even believe in binding arbitration. "It is not appropriate to public education," it said, because it takes away from the common interests of children, parents, teachers, and administrators.)

These same concerns had been expressed since teacher militancy flared up in the 1960s. "These organizations, teacher groups, seem to be seeking a power that would weaken lay control of education by usurping the policy-making functions of boards of education and the administrative responsibilities delegated by boards to superintendents," said the *Bulletin* of the Council for Basic Education in 1968. "If the boards are going to have the legal responsibility for running the schools, the boards must have the decision-making authority that will stick," said the executive director of the National School Boards Association in 1967.

210

The issue was put into perspective in 1968 by the executive secretary of the NEA Professional Rights and Responsibilities Commission. He said:

No public agency can survive and flourish without the confidence and goodwill of the public. Some skirmishes may be won by table pounding and belligerency and dogged insistence in looking at only one side of a controversy, but the public soon tires of seemingly unending battling without major advancement. . . . When the demands appear to be selfish or for gaining of personal power by purported leaders, confidence and goodwill rapidly approach the vanishing point. . . . The long-term support of the public is jeopardized everytime there is unreasonable action by school people—teachers, administrators, or boards of education. Our greatest hope for more than temporary gains depends upon our ability to secure and merit the goodwill, the friendly interest, and the informed support of the majority of the citizens of our nation.

Teacher-school board bargaining in itself can be a deterrent to the disruption of strikes when, by the very nature of what is negotiated, the dialogue leads to greater teacher professionalism. As early as the 1967–68 school year, teachers were negotiating for professional growth and/or in-service training; now they may achieve that status by first learning how to act like militant trade unionists—securing the economic base that will allow them to concentrate on professional problems. The flat assertion that teachers organize only to get money for themselves is a false one. Although, in fact, economic injustice was and is a basic cause of teacher militancy, other concerns of the teacher, including concern for better teaching conditions and a larger voice in educational decision making, play a central part. In oversimplified form, here is what happens when teachers become organized. First they achieve a contract, a say in the school system. Second they win salary equity. Then they begin to work on the basic problems of their school lives—the class load, the curriculum, the working conditions. The teacher's abiding interest in the negotiation process lies in this area of school improvement, once salary equity has been won and is on a continuing basis.

Increased militancy aids teacher morale. Collective bargaining increases the average teacher's personal feeling of security, both financial and otherwise. His morale is enhanced by the satisfaction and dignity resulting from the formal admission of him or his representatives to the decision-making process. And his ego is boosted by the knowledge that his professional aspirations and grievances and those of his colleagues must be given serious and formal consideration at the top level.

It is axiomatic, too, that negotiation leads to an enlarged role for teachers. The work of a researcher, Thomas M. Love, demonstrates this forcefully. Love examined questionnaires filled out by superintendents and assistant superintendents in school systems which had NEA or AFT affiliates as exclusive bargaining agents and in systems with no such agent. He found a dramatic increase by teachers in decision making when negotiation came on the scene. He reported:

In systems without collective negotiation teacher involvement is greatest in the area of educational policies, followed by salary matters and by a few other personnel policies. Many personnel policies are decided by the superintendent or the school board without any participation by teachers. . . . The establishment of collective negotiation enlarges the scope of teacher participation in decision making and also changes some of the decision processes. It enlarges the scope of teacher participation by reducing the extent of unilateral decision making by employers and by stimulating teacher organizations into more vigorous activity. The stimulus of collective negotiation is indicated by the fact that much more extensive proposals for policy changes are submitted by teachers with exclusive representation rights than by teachers without such rights.

Some have even suggested that collective bargaining would revitalize the role of the public school teacher in America. Charles S. Benson, who studied economic problems of education in the 1960s, noted:

Collective negotiation establishes a legally sanctioned confrontation of teachers face to face with members of the governing boards,

212

and this new practice can not fail to raise the teacher's professional self-image. . . . I feel it very likely that this kind of revitalization of the teacher's role will lead to a large increase in teacher-initiated innovation, not innovation imposed from above and implying a change in structure (team teaching, ungraded primary, and the like) but innovation occurring in the existing instructional situation and dealing with a fairly specific act of learning (teaching mathematics to disadvantaged elementary pupils by the "discovery methods").

LEGAL RIGHTS OF TEACHERS

Although the major gain to American teachers through organizing has been access to collective bargaining, other mechanisms have opened to them. One is the court suit. Alone, the teacher was unlikely to sue his school district if he was fired or mistreated. Organized, the teacher had access to union lawyers, to large defense funds, and to staff who pursued legal rights for him. As noted in chapter 12, hundreds of teachers were going into the courts each year by the mid-1970s.

Further, suits by teachers were setting precedents that saved other teachers from the same type of unfair treatment. In 1974 alone, unions won cases involving such wide-ranging issues as the right of pregnant teachers to remain in the classroom, the right of faculty to speak freely about college problems, and the right of a teacher to deduct home office expenses on his income-tax form. Other cases in that one year prevented school boards from infringing on teachers' free speech, blocked the use of test scores as the sole reason for firing teachers, and guaranteed that teachers could negotiate about such issues as student discipline, teacher load, and class size.

These suits have been so successful, and teacher unions have won so much membership support because of them, that it is unlikely they will stop. Both NEA and AFT were maintaining and building their defense funds in the 1970s; legal defense of rights had become a permanent part of the organized teachers' armor.

213

POLITICAL CLOUT

Another area of growing teacher effort in the 1970s was politics.

"Teacher Action Sweeps Friends of Education into Office," NEA told its members following the 1974 Congressional elections. "Pro-education and labor-backed candidates were swept into office in record number," AFT said. Both national groups had organized campaigns to help ensure that foes of school budgets and foes of teacher bargaining were kept out of Washington.

And they were looking ahead to 1976, when a new President would be chosen. AFT normally backed a national Presidential candidate; this time NEA too had developed a mechanism to endorse a candidate and to fund his campaign—through its Political Action Committee. NEA Executive Director Terry Herndon flatly predicted: "Teachers will be one of the most formidable forces in choosing the next President of the United States."

The candidates were taking teacher support seriously. Dozens of them issued statements after the 1974 election, thanking teachers for their support and praising their political abilities. They also thanked teachers for their financial support: during the 1974 election, AFT teachers gave about $1 million to candidates; NEA and its affiliates gave $2.5 million. Both groups were raising larger political war chests for 1976 and beyond.

Working with labor allies, continuing to build their political clout, teachers still have miles to go to gain the political influence other segments of American society have gained.

LOBBYING

A concomitant of teacher political clout is the

lobbying done by teacher unions in state capitals and in Washington.

Every one of NEA's state-level affiliates maintains a lobby in state legislatures; AFT staff are at work in states where there are large numbers of AFT members—Illinois, New York, Florida, California, Michigan, to name a few. Increased sophistication among these staffs, combined with increased membership and added political clout, guarantees an ever-growing state lobbying effort.

Nationally, NEA and AFT lobbyists in the 1970s were following hundreds of legislative issues—not only major school funding bills, but also other matters as wide ranging as voter registration, teacher retirement, veterans' educational benefits, copyright law, Indian education, unemployment compensation, and of course, collective bargaining. "Significant legislative support for public education" was one of NEA's six major goals in the 1970s; its 1975–76 budget alone allotted nearly two million dollars to achieve this goal. As teacher political power grows, feeding on its successes, this lobbying effort is likely to expand.

TEACHERS' SOCIAL GOALS

Teachers are idealists, and their organizations have tried to work for their ideals. Teacher organizers, sometimes remote from the classroom, often had to be reminded that teachers constantly see tomorrow; they want an improved society, better schools, equal rights, peace.

Thus, after teachers in a district are well organized, they begin to seek not just higher salaries and a more comfortable job situation; they have other, broader goals, such as bilingual education, desegregation, preschool education, women's rights, environmental education. Examine these statements:

"Bilingual programs could go a long way to make school truly reflect the joint AFT goals of democracy in education and education for democracy."—*American Teacher*

"The National Education Association believes that all citizens should be free to reside in the communities of their choice. Local affiliates should lead in breaking down barriers that limit this freedom."—an NEA resolution

"Current studies indicate that the public schools must assume an ever-larger role in providing positive 'conditions of life' for preschool children."—a 1974 teacher group report

"All schools teach sexism, but teachers can take the lead in changing stereotypes."—NEA staff member Shirley McCune

"The nation's priorities must include the protection of our environment."—an NEA task force

These expressions of concern reflect some of the spectrum of teacher awareness of social problems in the mid-1970s. How much influence teachers will have on these and other social issues is unknown, but it is clear that increasingly they are expecting their organizations to work on them.

The School Administrator

As teacher militancy grows, what happens to the school managers—the administrators, principals, curriculum developers? Basically, what happens to them is that they get pushed out of decision-making positions unless they become dedicated to the concerns and to the welfare of teachers.

In negotiations, teachers deal ultimately with the school board, not with the superintendent, who is left in a "go-between" position. AFT sees the superintendent as head of the opposition's negotiating team; NEA sees him as a member of the professional staff—at best a neutral catalyst providing resource information while NEA bargains with a board commit-tee or board attorney. School administrators' groups, not accepting this denigrated role for the superintendent, have said that "arbitrary action by either staff or school board is not likely to lead to lasting and satisfying resolution of disagreements."

If the school superintendent is questioning his role, so too is the school principal. Some point to the growing alienation of the principal from the organized classroom teacher. And there are other questions: Should such middle management personnel as principals be in the same negotiating unit with classroom teachers? Should they be on the administration negotiating team? When principals and department chairmen are excluded from the teacher's negotiations unit, should a separate unit be established for them?

NEA's president Alonso, himself a high school principal, suggested a new role for the principal. Classroom teachers expect the principal to be a curriculum innovator, he said in a speech before the National Association of Secondary School Principals.

> He will be expected to involve the whole faculty in curriculum development and to point out and to indicate new techniques, new methods, and new ideas. The principal will be looked upon as an expediter, one who should suggest how to do things more effectively. He will be expected to be a morale builder, to create a pleasant, wholesome atmosphere where learning will be a pleasure and teaching effective. The principal will be looked upon as a facilitator, one who will cut red tape, who will get things done. The principal will be looked upon as the delegator. The faculty knows we can't do everything. They expect us to trust them and delegate some authority. He will be expected to be an organizer. The principal will be looked upon as a coordinator, who will act as a team captain, not as a coach, where administration domination will be changed to cooperative efforts.

Others were not so optimistic. "Many argue that negotiation makes the principal a forgotten man," said an associate secretary of the American Association of School Administrators. Noting an erosion of principals' prerogatives, he said that individual principals might feel reduced in stature and importance. "This may be primarily a phenomenon of a given situation," he added. "It is not a reduction in the status of the principalship as a position. . . . The issue for the principalship is one of adjustment and reallocation of responsibilities—not of diminution of leadership importance."

The new role of the principal in some teachers' eyes may be inferred from this language in a negotiation agreement reached in Derby, Connecticut: "Each principal should be empowered to administer and supervise his building in the multitude of minor details that arise in the everyday operation of the plant and staff commensurate with his assigned authority and responsibility." Such descriptions confused principals and angered some of them. By 1975, many principals were talking about organizing their own collective bargaining units—one survey in 1975 showed that seven of ten elementary school principals wanted to go that route. But principals remained schizophrenic. They also considered themselves "management" and sided with the school administration; bargaining "against" the system would be hard for them.

Increased militancy by teachers also raised concern among curriculum development personnel. Where money is short, some asked, should salaries be raised at the expense, for example, of adequate services for emotionally disturbed children, curriculum development, integration programs, or other educational needs? Further, demands might be put forward by teacher groups for political rather than educational reasons. Militant action may result in the substituting of the political teacher for the master teacher as the key professional in the dynamics of a school or a district. Innovation may also be sacrificed to militancy, some feared, for it might be that teacher groups would seek to protect the status quo rather than sanction organizational or curricular changes. The teacher group intent on placating its membership so that it will not run the risk of losing to a rival union might resist educational innovation and halt the introduction of new teaching methods. As Anthony Oettinger says in *Run, Computer, Run*: "Innovation understandably fades before self-preservation."

Curriculum specialists, increasingly aware that more and more decisions about curriculum were being made through the bargaining contract, decided in 1975 to try to counter the trend toward the adversary relationship they felt they were being forced into as the result of bargaining. At the annual convention of the Association for Supervision and Curriculum Development, these subadministrators directed that the group develop a policy for involving curriculum specialists directly in the negotiation process. They sought a middle ground between teachers and top administrators, territory rapidly sinking from sight.

OTHER CHANGES

So the answer to the question, What is the future of teacher militancy? is partly that the trends of the 1960s and 1970s will continue. More collective bargaining agreements will be won and expanded by teachers, spelling out higher salaries and better working conditions. The mechanisms for teacher involvement in decision making will continue to grow, bringing more statewide bargaining laws, whether or not teachers and other public employees are brought under federal labor laws. Teachers will become more professional as bargaining provides for improved in-service training, more aides, better materials, and the like. Teacher morale should continue to increase as salaries rise (though inflation is a countering force) and as an expanded role in decision making continues to be won. School principals and administrators will suffer losses of power.

Strikes by teachers will eventually lessen as bargaining laws provide alternative means of solving disputes. But this does not necessarily assure that conflict between the public and the teacher will end. As the public becomes more aware of what schools are doing and not doing, new conflicts may arise.

In the 1960s, liberals of the Kennedy-Johnson mold convinced many Americans that social ills could be cured by spending more money. To the extent that the public accepted this concept, it accepted the demands of teachers for more money, for better (and more costly) school programs. But the bloom was off that particular lily by the mid-1970s. Expecting rapid improvement, the public saw instead minuscule results from more school costs. As with other social problems, solutions in education are difficult. For example, class size can make major differences in schooling. A skilled teacher who has only 10 pupils in an elementary classroom can work wonders in pupils' reading and calculating abilities, to mention just two areas of learning. But the school funding improvements of the 1960s and early 1970s rarely, if ever, involved reducing average elementary school class size to 10. Much more commonly the school budget increased vastly, teacher salaries went up, and class size dropped from 35 pupils to perhaps 33. Such changes are less than dramatic, and their results mean less than effective change. In fact, if at the same time the schools were given pupils who were less well prepared—children from homes less able to support them physically and psychologically—the achievement of the pupils in somewhat smaller classes might even be less. Parents are not likely to accept this situation. They are likely to conclude—and politically conservative segments of the society are likely to encourage them to conclude—that more money does not improve the schools.

This trend is reinforced by school critics of the 1970s (ironically, mostly on the political left). Authors such as Illich and Kozol, though mostly unread by the public, nevertheless strengthen the idea that the schools are not doing the job they should. And, to be sure, the school critics are right in one fundamental sense. The schools cannot, in and of themselves, solve the problems of society. Americans have always expected too much of their schools. They have even believed romantically that the schools have done more than they have. The ability of the public school to educate the immigrant, for instance, has been overblown. For every non-English-speaking immigrant child educated in the schools there were two who never entered, or, if they did, soon dropped out, spending their youth in the factory or on the street.

On top of this misunderstanding is the fact that the schools are expected to accomplish even more today. A larger number of children must be prepared for college in a range of disciplines that are ever more sophisticated. Imagine, for instance, the learning needs of a youth planning a career in space medicine or undersea engineering. And a wider range of children are entering the public schools with the expectation that they will receive an education. The courts have ruled, for example, that retarded but trainable children must be served by the schools, as must the physically handicapped. Further, there is the continuing societal problem of dealing with outcast urban children who face racial prejudice, generations of welfare, and family situations less than conducive to education. They are still pouring into the public classrooms. So our schools are being asked to do more at the same time that society seems to distrust the ability of the schools. This ironic situation could lead to worsened relations between teachers and their organizations, on the one hand, and parents and their representatives, on the other. Such a conflict is unlikely to make teachers less militant. It will, if anything, drive them further into the arms of protecting unions and associations.

MERGER AT LAST?

Meanwhile, another trend is evident, a trend toward some kind of consolidation of teacher groups. Although the National Education Association and the American Federation of Teachers broke off negotiations toward merger in 1974, it is probable that pressures building within these organizations will force some sort of teacher unity. It is unlikely, for example, that Albert Shanker, the AFT president, will suddenly forego his continuing push to organize all teachers. It is equally unlikely that NEA leaders will forever allow the AFT to drain away their members piecemeal through AFT campaigns to merge with state and local affiliates of the association.

The flow of history remains toward the eventual teacher unity predicted by both AFT leader Shanker and NEA leader Terry Herndon. Shanker said in 1974 that unity might come by the end of the decade; in 1973 Herndon said, "Ultimately the

AFT will be a part of the coordinated effort of all public employees." One possible scenario, for example, could result in a much larger power base for teachers because of the common purposes of teachers and other public employees. In the early 1970s, NEA and several public employee unions had already joined in a coalition working toward common goals called the Coalition of American Public Employees. Although AFT refused to join that coalition, the possibility remained that another coalition could be organized (through the AFL-CIO, for instance, which in 1974 established a Public Employees Council). With both NEA and AFT teachers represented in coalitions with other public employees, the question of merger could become a technicality; the changing structure of unions in the nation might, for example, lead to the separation of public employees from the AFL-CIO, with the American Federation of State, County, and Municipal Employees leading the way. In such a situation, the question of AFL-CIO affiliation might become academic. This scenario would result in an AFL-CIO of blue-collar and white-collar industrial and sales workers and a comparable national public employee federation of teachers, policemen, government workers, doctors, and nurses. Both national groups would have huge power, and each would be large enough to function outside the other.

Should such a combination succeed or not, one conclusion is inescapable: Teachers are not likely to stand alone again. Whether joined with other public employees as NEA proposes or joined with organized labor as AFT proposes, teachers will stand allied. Practioners of the craft of teaching no longer can turn inward; their future is enmeshed with other workers, other professionals.

From this and from other results of their militancy, teachers cannot escape. Their militancy will not halt, for despite their long struggle from genteel poverty to a meaningful role in American society, teachers continue to serve beneath their capacities. They remain relatively poorly paid. Their median salary was $11,000 in 1974, not high for a profession whose members increasingly need graduate degrees. Along with other public employees, they have a high moonlighting rate (about 15 percent of teachers hold a second job). Although the majority of teachers are organized, several hundred thousand remain unrecruited by unions or associations. Many teachers, too, are merely on the fringes of activism, their consciousnesses yet unraised, their faith in their own abilities to solve social problems undeveloped. Truck drivers can earn more money than teachers—and without moonlighting. Electricians are better organized. Doctors and nurses have a clearer sense of mission. As teachers enter the third century of the nation's history, they have room to grow, space for expansion before them. No one who has watched their history—especially the past 20 years—can expect their future to be less dynamic than their past.

Bibliography of Major Sources

CHAPTER 1

BARNARD, Henry (ed.). *American Journal of Education*, I (March, 1856), 304.
BARNARD, Henry (ed.). *American Journal of Education*, IV (March, 1858), 640.
BARNARD, Henry (ed.). *American Journal of Education*, V (September, 1858), 331; 787.
BUTTS, R. Freemen and Lawrence A. Cremin. *A History of Education in American Culture*. New York: Holt, Rinehart and Winston, 1953.
CLOUD, Roy W. *Education in California*. Stanford, Calif.: Stanford University Press, 1952.
ILLINOIS EDUCATION ASSOCIATION. *The History of the Illinois Education Association*. Springfield: the Association, 1961.
MOFFITT, John Clifton. *A Century of Service 1860–1960, A History of the Utah Education Association*. Salt Lake City: Utah Education Association, 1961.
NATIONAL TEACHERS ASSOCIATION. *NTA Proceedings*. Chicago: the Association, 1865.

CHAPTER 2

BRUBACHER, John S. *A History of the Problems of Education*. 2nd ed. New York: McGraw-Hill Book Co., 1966.
FENNER, Mildred Sandison. *The National Education Association, Its Development and Program*. Washington, D.C.: National Education Association, 1950.
HOLT, Andrew David. *The Struggle for a State System of Public Schools in Tennessee*. New York: Teachers College, Columbia University, 1938.

HUNKINS, Ralph V. *SDEA: The First Seventy-Five Years.* Pierre: South Dakota Education Association, 1958.

JOHNSON, Laurence B. *NJEA: The Story of an Organization.* Trenton: New Jersey Education Association, 1953.

LORD, Charles A. *Years of Decision 1865–1965: A History of the West Virginia Education Association.* Charleston: West Virginia Education Association, 1966.

NATIONAL EDUCATION ASSOCIATION. *NEA Proceedings.* Washington, D.C.: the Association, 1894.

WESLEY, Edgar B. *NEA: The First Hundred Years.* New York: Harper and Brothers, 1957.

ZISKIND, David. *One Thousand Strikes of Government Employees.* New York: Columbia University Press, 1940.

CHAPTER 3

ALEXANDER, Carter. *Some Present Aspects of the Work of Teachers' Voluntary Associations in the United States.* New York: Teachers College, Columbia University, 1910.

The American Teacher, I (January, 1913).

The American Teacher, I (February, 1913).

The American Teacher, V (February, 1916).

THE COMMISSION ON EDUCATIONAL RECONSTRUCTION. *Organizing the Teaching Profession: The Story of the American Federation of Teachers.* Glencoe, Ill.: The Free Press, 1955.

CRAWFORD, Albert Byron. "A Critical Analysis of the Present Status and Significant Trends of State Education Associations of the United States," *Bulletin of the Bureau of School Service,* University of Kentucky, IV (June, 1932), 35.

GOSS, Charles E. "Before the AFT: The Texas Experience," *Changing Education,* I (Summer, 1966), 6–9.

GRANRUD, John. *The Organization and Objectives of State Teachers' Associations.* New York: Teachers College, Columbia University, 1926.

HART, Irvin H. *Milestones: A History of the Iowa State Education Association, 1854–1945.* Des Moines: Iowa State Education Association, 1954.

MARSH, Arthur L. *The Organized Teachers.* Boston: the National

Association of Secretaries of State Education Associations, 1936.

NATIONAL EDUCATION ASSOCIATION. *NEA Proceedings*. Washington, D.C.: the Association, 1904.

———. *NEA Proceedings*. Washington, D.C.: the Association, 1905.

———. *NEA Proceedings*. Washington, D.C.: the Association, 1906.

———. *NEA Proceedings*. Washington, D.C.: the Association, 1907.

———. *NEA Proceedings*. Washington, D.C.: the Association, 1915.

NATIONAL EDUCATION ASSOCIATION, Research Division. *Achievements and Services of the State Education Associations*. Washington, D.C.: the Association, 1964.

OAKES, Russell Curtis. "Public and Professional Reactions to Teachers' Strikes, 1918–1954." Doctoral dissertation, New York University, 1958.

PETERSON, Florence. *Strikes in the United States 1880–1936*. Bulletin No. 651 (August, 1937). Washington, D.C.: U.S. Bureau of Labor Statistics.

ZITRON, Celia Lewis. *The New York City Teachers Union 1916–1964*. New York: Humanities Press, 1968.

CHAPTER 4

CHAMBERLAIN, Arthur H., and Richard G. Boone. *A Study of State Teachers Association*. San Francisco: Educational Press Association of America, 1922.

EDUCATIONAL POLICIES COMMISSION. *A National Organization for Education*. Washington, D.C.: the Commission, 1964.

EVERETT, Ruth Vick. "From Regimentation to Self-Government in the North Carolina Education Association And—Back Again." Unpublished document, The University of North Carolina, Chapel Hill, N.C., 1942.

GRAYBIEL, John M. "The American Federation of Teachers, 1916–1928." Master's thesis, University of California, 1928.

LYND, Robert S., and Helen Merrell. *Middletown, A Study in Contemporary American Culture*. New York: Harcourt, Brace and Co., 1929.

MESIROW, David. "The AFT's Role in the Thirties," *Changing Education*, I (Summer, 1966), 30–32.

NATIONAL EDUCATION ASSOCIATION. *NEA Proceedings.* Washington, D.C.: the Association, 1921.

————. *NEA Proceedings.* Washington, D.C.: the Association, 1925.

"A National Union Emerges," *Changing Education,* I (Summer, 1966), 11.

CHAPTER 5

CAMPBELL, Roald F., Luvern L. Cunningham, and Roderick F. McPhee. *The Organization and Control of American Schools.* Columbus, Ohio: Charles E. Merrill, 1965.

COUNTS, George S. "Socio-Economic Forces in Teachers' Strikes." *Phi Delta Kappan,* XXXVIII (April, 1947), 350–52.

GREGG, Russell T. and Roland A. Koyen. "Teachers Associations, Organizations, and Unions," *Review of Education Research,* XIX (June, 1949), 260–61.

LIEBERMAN, Myron. *Education as a Profession.* Englewood Cliffs, N.J.: Prentice-Hall, 1956.

"A New Era for Teachers, The Fifties and Sixties," *Changing Education,* I (Summer, 1966), 35–37.

SCHNAUFER, Pete. *The Uses of Teacher Power.* Chicago: The American Federation of Teachers, 1966.

SPALDING, Willard B., "Teachers' Organizations Are Poor Stuff," *Nation's Schools,* XXXVIII (March, 1946), 41–43.

CHAPTER 6

AMERICAN CIVIL LIBERTIES UNION, New York City Chapter. *The Burden of Blame.* New York: the Chapter, 1968.

FELDMAN, Sandra. *The Burden of Blame-Placing.* New York: United Federation of Teachers, 1969.

GOLDBLOOM, Maurice J. *The New York School Crisis.* New York: Commentary Reports, 1969.

LEVINE, Naomi, with Richard V. Cohen. *Ocean Hill-Brownsville: School in Crisis.* New York: Popular Library, 1969.

MAYER, Martin. *The Teachers Strike, New York, 1968.* New York: Harper and Row, 1969.

"N.Y. Teachers Battle for Due Process," *The American Teacher*, LIII (October, 1968), 4.

Ravitch, Diane. *The Great School Wars, New York City, 1805–1973*. New York: Basic Books, Inc., 1974.

Stinnett, T.M. *Turmoil in Teaching*. New York: Macmillan Co., 1968, p. 47.

Chapter 7

National Education Association. *Comparison of AFT Member-ship by States And Locals, 1962, 1963, and 1964*. Washington, D.C.: National Education Association, [n.d.] (distributed in January, 1965.)

———. *NEA Proceedings*. Washington, D.C.: the Association, 1961.

———. *NEA Proceedings*. Washington, D.C.: the Association, 1962.

———. *NEA Proceedings*. Washington, D.C.: the Association, 1963.

National Education Association, Office of Professional Development and Welfare. *Guidelines for Professional Negotiation*. Washington, D.C.: the Association, 1963.

Chapter 8

Beadle, June A. "Why I Resigned. . . ," *Impact* [Massachusetts Teacher Association] (March, 1968), 3.

Cass, James. "Politics and Education in the Sunshine State," *Saturday Review* (April 20, 1968), 63–65; 76–79.

Evans, John C., Jr. *Utah School Crisis 1963*. Salt Lake City: Utah Education Association, 1963.

National Education Association, Division of Press, Radio and Television Relations. "Florida Teachers Launch National Drive To Tell Truth About Florida School Crisis." Press release, March 18, 1968.

———. Memorandum to writers and broadcasters, February 26, 1968.

———. "NEA Votes $2 Million for Florida School Crisis." Press release, March 2, 1968.

Norton, Gayle E. "The Florida Story: An Evaluation." Speech at the annual meeting of the American Association of School Administrators, Atlantic City, New Jersey, February 15, 1967.

"Victory by Florida Teachers Among Most Significant in School History," *NEA Reporter*, VII (April 19, 1968), 1.

Chapter 9

Callahan, John J., William H. Wilkin, and M. Tracy Sillerman. *Urban Schools and School Finance Reform: Promise and Reality.* Washington, D.C.: National Urban Coalition, 1974.

Cogen, Charles. "Conservatism or Militancy," *The American Teacher*, L (February, 1966), 16.

"College Unionism . . . A Big Leap Forward," *The American Teacher*, LI (January, 1967), 9.

"Kansas City, Mo., Teachers Hold One-Day Walkout," *The American Teacher*, LI (October, 1966), 4.

"Militant Convention Action Spells Out Stronger Role for Future of Association," *NEA Reporter*, VI (July 21, 1967), 2.

National Education Association. *NEA Proceedings.* Washington, D.C.: the Association, 1966.

——. *NEA Proceedings.* Washington, D.C.: the Association, 1968.

National Education Association Research Division. *Withdrawals of Service by Teachers, January, 1940 to July, 1966.* Washington, D.C.: the Association, Urban Research Series, August, 1966.

"Teachers Win in California's First School Strike," *The American Teacher*, LI (October, 1966), 4.

Chapter 10

"ALMA-NASLRA Conference Devotes Full Time to Employer-Employee Relations in Government," *Government Employee Relations Report* (September 2, 1968), 30.

American Association of School Administrators. *The School Administrator and Negotiation.* Washington, D.C.: the Association, 1968.

An act repealing Section 175 of Article 77 of the Annotated Code of Maryland (1965 Replacement Volume), title "Public Education," subtitle "Chapter 15, Teachers' Associations, regarding the promotion of teachers' associations by the county examiners, and to enact new Section 175 in lieu thereof."

DASHIELL, Dick. *Report on Seventh Constitutional Convention, American Federation of Labor and Congress of Industrial Organizations*. Washington, D.C.: National Education Association, Division of Field and Urban Services, [n.d.] (The convention was held December, 1967.)

"Dismissal of Challenge to 'Agency Shop' Provision of Association's Contract with Warren, Michigan Schools," *Negotiation Research Digest* [National Education Association], II, No. 2, pp. c–8–11.

"Iowa Court Sees No Bar to Collective Bargaining by Public Employees," *Government Employee Relations Report*, July, 1968.

NATIONAL EDUCATION ASSOCIATION, Research Division. *Negotiation Agreement Provisions, 1966–67 Edition*. Washington, D.C.: the Association, 1967.

"No Conflict Seen Between Tenure Law and Agency-Shop Agreement," *The American Teacher*, LIII (November, 1968), 11.

OFFICE OF PROFESSIONAL NEGOTIATIONS, Michigan Education Association. *Special MEA Report*. Lansing: the Office, April, 1968.

"100,000 Teachers Now Serve Under Professional Negotiation Agreements in 346 U.S. Districts," *NEA Reporter*, III (November 20, 1964), 1, 8.

RASKIN, A. H. "How To Avoid Strikes by Garbagemen, Nurses, Teachers, Subway Men, Welfare Workers, etc.," *The New York Times Magazine*, February 25, 1968, pp. 34–36.

REDFERN, George D. "Negotiation Changes Principal-Teacher Relationships," *The National Elementary Principal*, XLVII (April, 1968), 25–27.

School District for the City of Holland, Ottawa and Allegan Counties, Michigan, v. Holland Education Association, Winona, Penna., Ted Boeve, Margaret Depress, Dorothy Bradish, Barbara Lampen, Della Bownman, John Doe and Mary Doe. Decision of the Supreme Court of the State of Michigan, 1968.

U.S. COURT OF APPEALS FOR THE SEVENTH CIRCUIT, Ruling on *James McLaughlin, et. al., v. Albert Tilendis, et al. Negotiation Research Digest*, II (January, 1969), C1–C2.

CHAPTER 11

"AFT and the College," *The American Teacher*, XI (May, 1966), 8.

AMERICAN FEDERATION OF TEACHERS. *AFT Officers' Reports to American Federation of Teachers Convention, 1967.* The Federation, 1967.

ASHBY, Lyle W. "Unity of the Profession: Why NEA Declined Union Member Proposal," *NEA Reporter*, VII (December 13, 1968), 2.

BLOOM, Arnold M. "A More Militant Profession," *American School and University*, XXXVII (October, 1964), 17.

"Clearinghouse: Urban Associations' Information-Exchange," *Urban Reporter* [NEA Urban Project], III (May–June, 1965), 2.

COGEN, Charles. Speech at annual convention of the American Federation of Teachers, Los Angeles, August 23, 1965.

DASHIELL, Dick. *Report of 52nd Annual Convention, American Federation of Teachers.* Washington, D.C.: National Education Association, Division of Field Services, [n.d.] (Convention held August, 1968.)

"Detroit Teachers Negotiate Pay Raise, Other Benefits," *White Collar Report*, September 10, 1964.

"EA Officer Sees Merger Likely with AFT 'Within 10 Years,'" *The American Teacher*, LIII (January, 1969), 5.

EDUCATIONAL POLICIES COMMISSION. *The Public Interest in How Teachers Organize.* Washington, D.C.: the Commission, 1964.

"Injunctions and Suit Delay Collective Bargaining Election," *Chicago Union Teacher*, XXXI (October, 1965), 6–9.

"IUD Subsidizes Drive to Organize California State College Faculties," *White Collar Report*, February 11, 1965.

NATIONAL EDUCATION ASSOCIATION. *NEA Proceedings.* Washington, D.C.: the Association, 1964.

————. *NEA Proceedings.* Washington, D.C.: the Association, 1966.

————. *Does Union Membership Mean Higher Salaries for Teachers?* Washington, D.C.: the Association [Urban Research Series], April, 1966.

NATIONAL EDUCATION ASSOCIATION, National Commission on Professional Rights and Responsibilities. *AFT Membership and Affiliated Locals, 1963–65.* Washington, D.C.: the Association, 1965.

NATIONAL EDUCATION ASSOCIATION, Division of Urban Services. *AFT Membership by States and Locals, 1965–66.* Washington, D.C.: the Association, [n.d.].

"NEA Membership Tops One Million," *NEA Reporter*, VI (April 21, 1967), 1.

"NEA 'Old Lady' Is 'Spry Chick' Labor Columnist Riesel Reports," *NEA Report*, VI (October 29, 1967), 7.

"NEA Rejects Union Bid for Talks on Merger," *NEA Reporter*, VII (October 25, 1968), 1.

NATIONAL EDUCATION ASSOCIATION, Salary Consultant Service. *Breakdown of Professional Negotiation Agreements on File at NEA, Revision No. 1*. Washington, D.C.: the Association, November 4, 1964.

NEW YORK STATE UNITED TEACHERS. *New York Teacher*, XVI (April 13, 1975), magazine section.

"Private Schools Chapter Steps Up Organizing Drive, Pact Negotiations," *The United Teacher* [of the New York City Federation of Teachers], February 4, 1965.

"308 Districts Have Agreed to Negotiation," *NEA Reporter*, IV (September 17, 1965), 6.

"Teacher Elections Across Nation Reveal Overwhelming Support for Professional Associations," *NEA Reporter*, IV (December 17, 1965), 1.

"Teacher Unity: An Overriding Goal," President's column, *The American Teacher*, LIII (September, 1968), 3.

CHAPTER 12

NATIONAL EDUCATION ASSOCIATION. *NEA Launches a New Decade of Action, 1969–1970 Annual Report*. Washington, D.C.: the Association, 1970.

——. *NEA Vital Force for Action, 1970–1971 Annual Report*. Washington, D.C.: the Association, 1971.

NATIONAL EDUCATION ASSOCIATION, Division of Teacher Rights. "NEA Actions on Behalf of Black Educators, 1966–1973," Washington, D.C.: the Association, [n.d.].

"When the Rights of Teachers Are Challenged, NEA Is There," *NEA Reporter*, XIV (May, 1975), 5.

CHAPTER 13

BLUM, Albert A. *Teachers Unions and Associations: A Comparative Study.* Urbana, Ill.: University of Illinois Press, 1969.

CASS, James and Max Birnbaum. "What Makes Teachers Militant," *Saturday Review,* LI (January 20, 1968), 54.

CORWIN, Ronald G. "Teacher Militancy in the United States: Reflections on Its Sources and Prospects," *Theory Into Practice,* VII (April, 1969), 99–100.

COUNTS, George S. "Socio-Economic Forces in Teachers' Strikes," *Phi Delta Kappan,* XXXVIII (April, 1947), 350.

CURTI, Merle. *The Social Ideas of American Educators,* Rev. Paterson, N.J.: Littlefield, Adams and Co., 1963.

DOHERTY, Robert E. (ed.). *Employer-Employee Relations in the Public Schools.* Ithaca, N.Y.: Cornell University School of Industrial and Labor Relations, 1967.

ELAM, Stanley. "Organizing the Teachers," *The Nation,* June 29, 1964, p. 14.

GARDNER, John W. *No Easy Victories.* New York: Harper and Row, 1968, p. 73.

LEVINE, Naomi, with Richard V. Cohen. *Ocean Hill-Brownsville: School in Crisis.* New York: Popular Library, 1969.

MOORE, William J. and Ray Marshall. "Growth of Teachers' Organizations: A Conceptual Framework," *Collective Negotiations in the Public Sector,* II (Summer, 1973), 271.

NATIONAL EDUCATION ASSOCIATION, National Commission on Teacher Education and Professional Standards. *Milestones.* Washington, D.C.: the Association, 1966.

NOLTE, M. Chester. "Next Finger in the Collective Bargaining Pie May Be on a Federal Hand," *American School Board Journal,* CLVI (February, 1969), 24–25.

ROSENTHAL, Allan. "The Strength of Teacher Organizations: Factors Influencing Membership in Two Large Cities," *Sociology of Education,* XXXIX (Fall, 1966), 359–380.

SCHIFF, Albert. "A Study and Evaluation of Teachers' Strikes in the United States." Doctoral dissertation, Wayne University, 1952.

STAR, Jack. "Our Angry Teachers," *Look,* September 3, 1968, p. 14.

STINNETT, T.M. *Turmoil in Teaching.* New York: Macmillan Co., 1968, p. 4.

WOODRING, Paul. "On the Causes of Teacher Discontent," *Saturday Review*, L (October 21, 1967), 61.

CHAPTER 14

AMERICAN ASSOCIATION OF SCHOOL ADMINISTRATORS. *Roles, Responsibilities, Relationships of the School Board, Superintendent, and Staff.* Washington, D.C.: the Association, 1963.

DASHIELL, Dick. *Report on the 35th Annual Convention of the National School Boards Association.* Washington, D.C.: National Education Association, Division of Affiliate Services, [n.d.] (Convention held April 19–22, 1975).

DOHERTY, Robert E. (ed.). *Employer-Employee Relations in the Public Schools.* Ithaca, N.Y.: Cornell University School of Industrial and Labor Relations, 1967.

DOHERTY, Robert E. and Walter E. Oberer. *Teachers, School Boards, and Collective Bargaining: A Changing of the Guard.* Ithaca, N.Y.: Cornell University School of Industrial and Labor Relations, 1967.

DOHERTY, Robert E. and others (eds.). *The Changing Employment Relationship in Public Schools.* Ithaca, N.Y.: Cornell University School of Industrial and Labor Relations, 1966.

HIRSCH, Werner Z. and others. *Inventing Education for the Future.* San Francisco: Chandler Publishing Co., 1967, p. 346.

LIEBERMAN, Myron. "Collective Negotiations: Status and Trends," *American School Board Journal*, CLV (October, 1967), 8.

NATIONAL EDUCATION ASSOCIATION. *1969 NEA Convention Report.* Washington, D.C.: the Association, 1969.

———. *The Public Employee: Do We Need a Federal Law To Guarantee His Bargaining Rights?* Washington, D.C.: the Association, 1974.

"Negotiation Agreements: Qualifications for Professional Growth and In-Service Training," *Negotiation Research Digest*, II (May, 1969), B1.

OETTINGER, Anthony G. *Run, Computer, Run.* Cambridge, Mass.: Harvard University Press, 1968, p. 64.

RHODES, Eric F. and Richard P. Long. *The Principal's Role in Collective Negotiations.* Washington, D.C.: Educational Service Bureau, Inc., 1967.

SHILS, Edward B. and C. Taylor Whittier. "The Superintendent, the School Board, and Collective Negotiations," *Teachers College Record*, LXIX (October, 1967), 61–65.

"The Way It Was: Education 1967," *Bulletin of the Council for Basic Education*, XII (January, 1968), 4.

Index

Boldface numbers refer to photographs.